Opus 42

Heinz Tesar
Christus Hoffnung der Welt, Wien

Text
Immo Boyken

Photographien/Photographs
Christian Richters

Edition Axel Menges

Herausgeber/Editor: Axel Menges

ISBN 3-930698-42-0

Reproduktionen/Reproductions: Kostal & Schindler OEG, Wien/Vienna
Druck/Printing: Druckhaus Münster GmbH, Kornwestheim
Bindearbeiten/Binding: Großbuchbinderei Josef Spinner GmbH, Ottersweier

Übersetzung ins Englische/Translation into English: Michael Robinson, London
Design: Axel Menges

Inhalt

Contents

Immo Boyken

Bescheidenheit im Überfluß – Heinz Tesars Kirche in der Wiener Donau City

»Entsprechend der Aufgabenstellung, eine Kirche an der Wende zum dritten Jahrtausend zu bauen, wurde diese in einem Teil der Stadt Wien errichtet, der das erklärte Ziel hat, dem historischen Zentrum jenseits der Donau ein Gegenüber zu geben«, schreibt Heinz Tesar, der Architekt. Erdrückende Vorgaben: Bauen auf der Jahrtausendschwelle und Konkurrierenmüssen mit dem historischen Zentrum Wiens, mit dem Stephansdom als heute immer noch wirksamer Stadtkrone, der Ringstraße mit ihren Prachtbauten und dem Heldenplatz, mit Fischer von Erlach, Hildebrandt, Theophil von Hansen, Gottfried Semper, Otto Wagner, Adolf Loos, mit weithin populärer Salonarchitektur an prominentester Stelle – fast zu übermächtige Signale für einen eigenen Beginn. Einen Weg in die falsche Richtung zu beschreiten, einem Drängen zu artistischer Architektur nachzugeben, »so recht gemacht, um der Masse mit sich selbst zu imponieren«, wie es Goethe formuliert, hätte nahegelegen, architektonische Spielereien, geboren aus einem gegebenen Zwang zu dröhnender Originalität, hätten sich wohl vermuten lassen, Originalität, die nach Alberti nur dann zu loben sei, wenn sie nicht zu Extravaganzen führe.

Artistisch und extravagant als Folge allzu hochgeschraubter Vorgaben und allzumächtigen Sich-von-der-Welt-beobachtet-Fühlens – die Beispiele sind Legion: der Eiffelturm als Symbol der Weltausstellung von 1889 und als welthöchstes Bauwerk überhaupt ist eigentlich ein – kühnes – Monstrum, an das man sich gewöhnt hat, das Atomium in Brüssel als Symbol der Weltausstellung von 1958 und als Abbild fortschrittlichen naturwissenschaftlichen Denkens und Handelns ist ebenso ein – weniger kühnes – Monstrum auf Krücken, an das man sich nicht gewöhnen mag, die einzelnen Ausstellungsbauten der Nationen verlieren sich, von wenigen Ausnahmen abgesehen – Henry van de Velde und Walter Gropius mit Adolf Meyer in Köln 1914, Mies van der Rohe in Barcelona 1929, Gunnar Asplund in Stockholm 1930, Egon Eiermann und Sep Ruf in Brüssel 1958, Sverre Fehn in Venedig 1962 – trotz zumeist klangvoller Namen, die damit verbunden sind, in mondäner Ausdruckstänzelei (auch Bruno Tauts Glaspavillon ist nicht frei davon), und Adolf Loos' berühmt-berüchtigte Säule für das Verwaltungsgebäude der *Chicago Tribune* von 1922 ist gleichsam aus diesen Voraussetzungen zu erklären, nämlich, wie es in der Wettbewerbsauslobung heißt, »to erect the most beautiful and distinctive office building in the world«; und dieser bemerkenswerten Forderung, das schönste und bedeutendste Bürogebäude der Welt zu errichten, glaubte Loos mit dorischer Architektur genügen zu können – ein Unikum das Ganze, das wohl nur deswegen nicht im Dunkel der Geschichte verschwunden ist, weil man es Loos, dem Architekten des »Raumplans«, des Hauses Steiner, des Cafés Museum, des Michaelerhauses – auch als möglicherweise bewußte Provokation – letztlich nicht zutrauen will.

Und hier? Die Schwelle zum neuen Jahrtausend also und die Donau City als Pendant zur Wiener Altstadt: jenseits von Donau und Donaukanal, sieben, acht U-Bahn-Minuten vom historischen Zentrum entfernt, liegt/steht die neue Stadt: eine Versammlung von Hochhäusern aller Arten, konvex und konkav geschwungen, kantig, oval, mit expressiver Zutat geschminkt, hohe Stempel, niedrigere Riegel, fladenartig-flache Bauten – von allem zuviel, das Abbild rastloser Geschäftigkeit; geordnet – geordnet? – um eine zugige Fläche, zu weiträumig und an ihren Raumkanten zu zerfleddert, um ein städtischer Platz zu sein, angeschnitten durch eine diagonal verlaufende Achse, die am Bus- und U-Bahnhof beginnt und sich, leicht ansteigend, irgendwo ins Leere verliert – geradeso als hätten die Stadtplaner Camillo Sitte gänzlich vergessen, als hätten sie die Stadtbaukunst zu einer Wissenschaft gemacht, mit der das, was nur Hilfe sein dürfte, zur Hauptsache geworden ist; der Verstand ist mehr angesprochen als das Gefühl, anstelle der Augen ist das Gehirn getreten, wie es Rilke in seinen *Duineser Elegien* sagt.

Was Frankfurt am Main wesentlich in seiner Mitte, was Paris am Ende der Avenue des Champs-Elysées und der in ihrer Flucht aufgefädelten Straßen hat, hat Wien nun am Rande der Stadt, ein Wohn-und Arbeitszentrum, das auf den Zustrom von 7000 bis 8000 Menschen ausgerichtet ist, appendixhaft an die Peripherie geheftet. Eine Massenansammlung, die keine Urbanität ausmacht, nicht zum Verweilen, nur zum Durcheilen einlädt.

Und mitten darin, nicht in geometrischer, aber doch in ideeller Mitte, liegt der Bauplatz der neuen Kirche, steht heute also Heinz Tesars Bau, klein in der Kubatur, groß in der Wirkung, ein Glücksfall für diesen neuen Stadtbezirk, der in die öde Leere eine neue Fülle bringt; eine Fülle nicht durch Auftrumpfen über die sich rundum aufbäumenden Kubaturen, nicht durch Eintags-Extravaganzen, durch formalistisches Getue oder effektheischende Schlenkereien, sondern durch eine unaufgeregte Geste, durch Bescheidenheit; eine Bescheidenheit allerdings von hintergründiger Raffinesse.

Die Kirche Christus Hoffnung der Welt stellt sich der Herausforderung, dieser modernen Neustadt in gewolltem Kräftebezug zur Wiener Altstadt durch die Umkehrung des Naheliegenden eine geistige Mitte zu geben; nicht die Kirche als Krönung der Stadt im Sinne der Tautschen Stadtkrone: der Tempel, die Kathedrale, der Dom, sondern die Kirche als kleinster Bau, eingehüllt von den erdrückenden Gesten der drumherumstehenden Stempel und Riegel. Und doch Stadtkrone: nicht das Untergehen wie die St. Patrick's Cathedral in New York, die wie ein verlorenes Relikt im Häusermeer steht und verliert, nicht wie Stülers Berliner Matthäuskirche, die sich – aus ihrem eigentlichen Zusammenhang gerissen – gegen Mies van der Rohes Nationalgalerie, Scharouns Philharmonie und die Fläche dazwischen behaupten muß und auch verliert. Stadtkrone durch die Kraft einer Miniatur, durch die Kraft des Leisen gegen das Laute, eine »Oase in der Diaspora«, um Karl Rahners Wort über die Gemeinden der Zukunft zu verwenden.

Der Bau der Kirche gibt sich schroff: ein harter, an den Ecken aufgebrochener Kubus, der mit schwarzfarbenen Chromstahlplatten belegt ist. Schroff auf den ersten Blick. Auf den zweiten wird die Härte verbindlich: durch die matten Spiegelungen, die das Material zuläßt; durch das Raster der großflächigen Platten, dem hellglänzende Bohrungen antworten, die die Wände wie ein feines Gespinst überziehen und die an eine weitreichende Wiener Tradition erinnern, an die Befestigungsbolzen, mit denen Otto Wagner die Steinplatten der Fassaden seines Postsparkassengebäudes und seiner Kirche am Steinhof deutlich sichtbar als nicht massiv,

Immo Boyken

Modesty in excess – Heinz Tesar's church in the Donau City in Vienna

»The brief was to build a church for the turn to the third millennium, and so it was built in a part of Vienna whose declared objective is to provide a counterpart to the historic centre on the other side of the Danube«, writes Heinz Tesar, the architect. An overwhelming brief: building on the threshold of the new millenium and having to compete with the historical centre of Vienna, with the Stephansdom, still the city's crowning glory, the Ringstraße with its magnificent buildings and the Heldenplatz, with Fischer von Erlach, Hildebrandt, Theophil von Hansen, Gottfried Semper, Otto Wagner, Adolf Loos, and with a great deal of straightforward popular architecture, in a highly exposed position – signals that are perhaps all too powerful when trying to make a start oneself. If Tesar had taken a step in the wrong direction, if he had given in to pressure to produce artistic architecture, »actually done to impress the masses with themselves«, as Goethe puts it, would have suggested architectural games, born of a compulsion to produce something resoundingly original, it would have evoked an originality that according to Alberti is only to be praised if it does not lead to extravagance.

Artistic and extravagant as a result of undue demand and of an overpowering sense that the eyes of the world are upon one – the examples are legion: the Eiffel Tower as a symbol of the 1889 World Fair and as the world's tallest structure is actually a – bold – monstrosity that people have got used to, the Atomium in Brussels as a symbol of the 1958 World Fair and as an image of progressive scientific thought and action is also a – less bold – monstrosity on crutches that people are not keen to get used to, individual national show buildings lose themselves, with a very few exceptions – Henry van de Velde and Walter Gropius with Adolf Meyer in Cologne in 1914, Mies van der Rohe in Barcelona in 1929, Gunnar Asplund in Stockholm in 1930, Egon Eiermann and Sep Ruf in Brussels in 1958, Sverre Fehn in Venice in 1962 – despite the largely illustrious names associated with them, these buildings lose themselves in mundane, expressive prancing (even Bruno Taut's glass pavilion is not free of this), and Adolf Loos's famous-infamous column for the *Chicago Tribune* offices in 1922 can effectively be explained by the requirements, in other words, as the exhibition brief said, »to erect the most beautiful and distinctive office building in the world« – and Adolf Loos thought that he would be able to do this with Doric architecture – a unique object overall, which has probably only avoided being lost in the darkness of history because ultimately no one is prepared to believe that Loos, the architect of the »Raumplan«, the Steiner House, the Café Museum, the Michaelerhaus could have been capable of it – even as a conscious provocation.

And here? The threshold of the new century and the Donau City as a companion piece to the old town in Vienna: on the other side of the Danube and the Danube canal, seven, eight minutes away from the historic centre by underground is this new town: an accumulation of high-rise buildings of all kinds, with convex and concave curves, angular, oval, adorned with expressive additions, tall prop, lower bar, flat, round buildings – too much of everything, the image of being ceaselessly busy; ordered – ordered? – around a draughty area that is too spacious and too tattered on its periphery to be an urban square, cut through by a diagonal axis that starts at the bus and underground station and gets lost – climbing slightly – in the midst of all the emptiness – just as though the town planners had completely forgotten Camillo Sitte, as though they had made urban architecture into a science that has turned something that should have been a mere aid into the main axis; the intellect is addressed rather than the feelings, the brain has taken over from the eyes, as Rilke says in his *Duineser Elegien*.

Vienna now has on its periphery something that Frankfurt am Main essentially has in its centre, that Paris has at the end of the Champs-Elysées and in the streets that have been threaded on to its sweep: a residential and working centre that is intended to accommodate 7000 to 8000 additional people, attached to its periphery like an appendix. A mass accumulation that does not create urban quality, and certainly does not invite people to linger, just to hurry through.

And in the middle of all this, not in the geographical but in the ideal centre, is the site for the new church, for Heinz Tesar's building, which is small in terms of cubature, large in the effect it makes, a happy event for this new urban district that brings a new sense of fullness to this empty desolation; and this is not a fullness created by showing its superiority to all the cubatures that are rearing up around it, not by any one-day wonder extravagance, formalistic fuss or attention-seeking frills, but by making a calm gesture, by being modest; but it is a modesty that shows cunning refinement.

The church of »Christ Hope of the World« addresses the challenge of providing a spiritual centre for this modern new town that stands in a deliberately forceful relationship with the old town of Vienna by reversing the obvious; not the church as the crown of the city in the sense implied by Taut: the temple, the cathedral, the dome, but the church as the smallest building, hidden by the overwhelming gestures made by the props and blocks around it. And yet it does crown the city: it is not submerged like St. Patrick's Cathedral in New York, which stand in the sea of buildings like a lost relic, and loses; it is not like Stüler's Matthäuskirche in Berlin which – ripped out of its actual context – has to hold its own against Mies van der Rohe's Nationalgalerie, Scharoun's Philharmonie and the area in between, and also loses. It is the crown of the city because it has the power of a miniature, the power of quietness set against noise, an »oasis in the diaspora«, to use Karl Rahner's phrase about the congregations of the future.

The structure of the church seems stark: a hard cube, broken open at the corners, covered with black chromium steel sheets. Stark at a first glance. On a second glance the hardness becomes friendly: because of the dull reflections that the material permits, because of the grid of broad sheets, to which the brightly gleaming drill-holes respond, covering the walls like a fine web and reminiscent of a long Viennese tradition, of the bolts that Otto Wagner used to fasten the stone slabs of his Postsparkasse building and of his Kirche am Steinhof, leaving them clearly visible to show that the stone is not solid but simply a cladding that is applied on the outside, bolts that are functional, but also (especially in the upper regions of the post-office building) a purely decorative element; because of the scattered circular apertures of two sizes that allow light to escape

sondern als nur vorgeblendete Verkleidung zeigt, Bolzen, die funktionales, aber auch (besonders in den oberen Regionen des Postgebäudes) rein dekoratives Element sind; durch eingestreute kreisrunde Öffnungen von zweierlei Größen, die bei Dunkelheit Licht nach außen strahlen lassen; durch große, rechteckige Fenster in den einspringenden Ecken, die Kontrast zum Geschlossenen schaffen; durch ein signifikantes, großes weißes Kreuz, das als einziger sichtbarer Schmuck in die Wand eingelassen ist; durch die Rahmung des Haupteingangs, die wie ein Profil frei vor der Wand steht; durch den Glockenträger, der im Abseits geduckt wie neben der Kirche steht und dem etwas Provisorisches eigen ist, als brauchte dieser Bau den Klang der Glocken eigentlich nicht.

Innen weicht das Schroffe ganz: ein lichter, heller, ein liebenswürdiger Raum, in den man durch ein elegant gestaltetes Entrée von kunstvoller Einfachheit hineingeleitet wird; eine eigentlich eher karge Raumhülle, die wesentlich durch das helle Material – Birkenholz – lebt, durch die ebenso lebendige wie ruhige Ordnung des Gestühls: verschieden große Kreissegmente, die den Altarblock aus dunklem Seynit in offener Kreisform umfassen und einen Zentralbau andeuten, und besonders durch die differenzierten Lichtquellen: die kreisrunden Öffnungen, die den introvertierten Innenraum transparent machen, die großen Fenster in den ausgesparten Ecken, die Lichtinseln schaffen, eine frei geformte Öffnung in der Decke, die Licht auf den Altar gleiten läßt und die ein Signum sein mag.

»Der Grundgedanke des Entwurfes ist es«, schreibt Tesar, »den Kirchenneubau durch die städtebauliche Konstellation des ›Über-die-Donau-Bringens‹ als Sakralbau am Platz als Auftakt zum neuen Stadtviertel zu verankern.« Das neue Stadtviertel: Außerhalb schon des nachwirkenden Kräftefeldes der Innenstadt entläßt einen die U-Bahn, die im Bereich der Donau City zur Hochbahn geworden ist – die Armut des Bahnhofs läßt einen wehmütig an Otto Wagners Stationen, ihre schöne, ebenso disziplinierte wie phantasiereiche Architektur denken –, über die Hindernisse von Straßen und Busparkschleifen, zwangsgeleitet durch einen Zebrastreifen, auf die »Diagonal-Achse«, eine rot asphaltierte Fußgänger-Erschließungsstraße, deren kreisrunde Kontur als Auftakt des Ganzen man kaum wahrnimmt, vielleicht eben noch als Geometrie erkennt, und deren räumliche Fassung durch einen viertelkreisförmigen Baukörper zwar schon spürbar ist, dessen Rolle als Ordnungsfaktor man aber ebenfalls kaum wahrnimmt – vielleicht mit dem Verstand, nicht aber mit dem Gefühl. Man möchte umkehren in die befreiende Dichte der Altstadt, wenn der Blick nicht gefangen würde durch diesen schwarzfarbenen Block mit dem hellen Kreuz als Signal, der aus dem Boden herauszuwachsen scheint und sich selbst gegen die Gewalt einer übermächtigen, fensterlosen Betonwand, eines der Erschließungsschächte des Uno-Gebäudes, behauptet.

Der erste Eindruck ist der: Schwarz, wie mir bedeutet wurde, schwarz ist dieser Quader nicht; im Gegenteil, er wirkt nicht einmal dunkel, selbst an einem weitgehend sonnenlichtlosen Tag nicht. Er changiert in vielen Farben, und er erinnert mich spontan an die Farben hamburgischer Klinkerbauten, besonders an die Fritz Högers mit seiner Vorliebe für Steine dritter Wahl und ihren verstärkt farblichen Unregelmäßigkeiten; und vielleicht haben auch die größeren und kleineren kreisrunden Störungen der Wände einen ihrer Ursprünge in Hamburg, im Überseehafen, im Erlebnis der am Pier liegenden großen Schiffe mit ihren hoch aufragenden Wandungen aus Stahl und den Bullaugen darin, oder in Högers und Gersons Sprinkenhof, dessen Fassaden mit vergoldeten Knäufen verziert sind, die Höger allerdings später als ein Zuviel nicht mehr gelten lassen wollte (Störungen, für die – als auslösendes Moment – auch das Klostergebäude der Franziskaner mitten in der Wiener Altstadt stehen mag, ein architektonisch eher anspruchsloser Bau, dessen Fassaden aber durch zahllose kreisrund gerahmte, farblich hervorgehobene Blindfenster geprägt sind und die hier dem Bau Charakter verleihen).

Bei Tesar, der in Hamburg als Ingenieur in einem Büro für Baustatik seinen Weg zu beschreiten begonnen hat, dem präzises, naturwissenschaftlich geprägtes Denken als Regulativ zu überquellender architektonischer Phantasie immer zur Seite steht, sind diese Störungen kein Zuviel. Im Gegenteil, sie geben diesem scheinbar harten, schweren Block etwas Leichtes, ja Unpathetisches, das auf das Innere vorwegweist. Auch ist dieser harte Block weder hart noch eigentlich Block, denn dem rein Kantigen antworten die Auskerbungen an allen vier Ecken in abgestuften Größen, und dem Blockhaften, dem Quader, antwortet ein sockelloses Eingesenktsein in den Boden, das suggeriert, betont durch eine horizontale Fuge (die zugleich die direkte und diskrete Belichtung der Gemeinderäume im Untergeschoß möglich macht), als stände der Bau nicht fest auf dem Boden, sondern wachse wie eine Art Pfeiler aus ihm heraus; wiederum vergleichbar dem Eindruck am Hafenrand angelandeter Schiffe, die mit wechselndem Wasserstand vor der Kaimauer auf- und niederwachsen.

Beim Näherkommen und Umrunden offenbart sich die Raffinesse: Die changierende Fassade besteht in ihrer sichtbaren Haut aus längsrechteckigen Chromstahlplatten, die nach einem berechneten Raster gefügt und ebenso berechnet mit Bohrungen und Öffnungen perforiert sind, »Naturlichtnotate«, wie Tesar sagt, die nur an einer Stelle aussetzen und eine – von den Bohrungen gleichwohl übergriffene – Fläche in der Fläche bilden, dort, wo im Inneren ein großer, kreisrunder Bezirk mit integriertem Kreuz intarsienartig in die Wand eingearbeitet ist und den Altarbezirk höht. Das Innere wird so außen vorbereitet, und vorbereitet wird es auch durch die bullaugenartigen Lichtöffnungen, die – wie gesagt, einem am Pier liegenden Schiff gleich – dem Aus-der-Erde-Herauswachsen entsprechend knapp über dem Boden beginnen und in verschiedenen Augenhöhen den Blick nach innen zulassen (und, deutlicher spürbar noch, von innen nach außen).

Der Block beginnt sockellos, steigt aus dem Grund auf, und er endet abrupt, scharfkantig, schnörkellos. Wieder das Bild des Schiffes, das Bild der Kommandobrücke mit seitlichen Auslegern, die hier gleichsam nach innen gerichtet sind: einer Kommandobrücke des Geistes, des Glaubens vielleicht, die überzeugt, weil das Kommando nicht hinausgeschrien wird, sondern durch Überzeugung Kraft hat. Und entsprechend einer Brücke, einem Schiffsaufbau ist auch die fünfte Ansicht dieses Quaders gestaltet, die zumeist architektonisch sträflich vernachlässigte Dachaufsicht, die hier an diesem Ort besonderes Gewicht erhält, weil sie von überall, von den Hochhäusern rundum, einsehbar ist. Nicht die übliche bekieste Fläche mit den obligaten üblen Stutzen der Haustechnik, nicht das begrünte Dach,

1. Fritz Höger mit Hans und Oskar Gerson, Sprinkenhof, Hamburg, 1927–43.
2. Abraham Mall, Franziskanerkloster, Wien, 1616–21.

1. Fritz Höger with Hans and Oskar Gerson, Sprinkenhof, Hamburg, 1927–43.
2. Abraham Mall, Franciscan monastery building, Vienna, 1616–21.

to the outside when it is dark; because of large rectangular windows in the set-back corners, which provide a contrast with the closed look; because of a significant large, white cross, let into the wall as the only visible decoration; because of the framing of the main entrance that stands freely in front of the wall like a profile; because of the belfry, crouching at the side as though it has nothing to do with the church, and looking so provisional that it seems to want to say that this building does not actually need the sound of bells.

The interior is not stark at all: a light, bright, amiable space. We are led into it through an artfully simple, elegantly designed entrance; a spatial envelope that is actually sparse in essence, drawing its life mainly from the light-coloured material – birch-wood – and from the arrangement of the pews: different-sized segments of a circle surrounding the dark seynite altar block in an open circle and suggesting a centrally-planned building, an impression that is reinforced especially by the sophisticated light sources: the circular apertures that render the introverted interior transparent, the large windows in the inset corners, which create islands of light, a freely-shaped aperture in the ceiling, which allows light to slip down on to the altar; it may be a sign.

»The basic idea behind the design«, writes Tesar, »is to anchor the new church by means of an urban constellation based on moving-across-the-Danube, a religious building as a prelude to the new urban quarter.« The new urban quarter: you are already beyond the after-effects of the force-field of the city centre when the underground, which has become an elevated railway in the Donau City area, lets you out – the poverty of the station makes you think of Otto Wagner's stations with some degree of melancholy, and their beautiful architecture that was as disciplined as it was imaginative – but it lets you out, via the obstacles of the roads and bus parking lanes, to be forced by a zebra crossing on to the »diagonal axis«, a red-asphalted pedestrian access road whose circular line you do not at first notice as a prelude to the whole complex, though perhaps just as a piece of geometry. Its spatial enclosure by a quarter-circular building is also scarcely perceptible – perhaps intellectually, but certainly not emotionally. You feel like going back into the liberating density of the old town, if your eye was not caught by this black block with the bright cross as a signal, seeming to grow out of the ground to assert itself against the violence of an excessively powerful concrete wall without windows, one of the access shafts to the Uno building.

The first impression is this: black, as I was informed, this cuboid is not black; on the contrary, it does not even seem dark, even on a day that is largely without sunlight. It is iridescent in many colours, and it spontaneously reminds me of the hue of clinker buildings in Hamburg, especially those by Fritz Höger with his preference for reject bricks with their increasingly irregular colours; and perhaps the larger and smaller circular interruptions of the walls may have one of their sources in the overseas port in Hamburg, in the experience of the big ships at the pier with their towering steel, portholed walls, or in Höger's and Gerson's Sprinkenhof, whose façades are decorated with gilded knobs, though Höger was later prepared to admit that they were too much (disruptions which – as an element of release – the Franciscan monastery building in the middle of the old town in Vienna might also represent, a building of no particular architectural distinction, but its façades draw their characteristic appearance from countless blind windows with circular frames, picked out in colour).

In Tesar's case – Tesar started his career in Hamburg as an engineer in a building statics office, and he always had precise scientific thinking on his side to balance overflowing architectural imagination – these disruptions are not too much. On the contrary, they give this apparently hard, heavy block a quality of lightness, indeed a lack of emotion and drama that anticipates the interior. And this hard block is actually neither hard nor a block, as the purely angular element is answered by the notches on all four corners, in staggered sizes, and the block-like quality, the cuboid, is answered by the fact that it is planted in the ground without a plinth, and this suggests, emphasized by a horizontal joint (that at the same time makes it possible to provide some direct and discreet illumination for the parish rooms in the basement), that the building is not standing firmly on the ground, but growing out of it like a kind of pillar; this is once again comparable with the impression given by ships anchored at the edge of the harbour, moving up and down again in front of the harbour wall with the rising and falling tide.

The refinement is revealed as you come closer and walk around the building: the outer skin of the iridescent façade consists of longitudinally rectangular chromium steel sheets placed according to a calculated grid and perforated with drill-holes and apertures, also precisely calculated. »Notes of natural light«, as Tesar says, that stop at one point only and form an area within the area – though the drill-holes still continue – and this is the point at which, inside the church, a large, circular section with an integrated cross is let into the wall like marquetry, intensifying the sanctuary. Thus the interior is anticipated in the exterior, and it is also anticipated by the porthole-like light apertures – as has been said, like a ship at its moorings. They correspond with the sense of growing out of the earth; starting just above ground level, they make it possible to look inside at various levels (and, even more clearly, to look outside from the inside).

The block starts without a plinth, rises up from the ground, and ends abruptly, sharp-edged, without any frills. Again the image of the ship, the image of the bridge with outriggers at the sides, which here are directed inwards, as it were; a bridge of the spirit, of faith perhaps; it is convincing because commands are not shouted from this bridge, but draw their power from conviction. And appropriately to a bridge, to the superstructure of a ship, the fifth aspect of this cuboid is designed to be seen, the top view, which is often culpably neglected by architects. It carries particular weight here because it can be seen from everywhere, from all the high buildings around it. It is not the usual gravel area with the obligatory hideous service pipe-ends, not a planted roof, trying to wrest back a token piece of nature, but an immaculate surface in the same material as the walls, the chromium steel sheets (though without their perforations here), from which a free form rises like a sculpture, the fanlight, indicating the position of the altar, and a joint running round the edge of the area, reminiscent of a kind of railing.

The entrance to the church is not placed directly on the line of approach that would be taken by someone coming from the bus or underground station, and it is also not underneath the great, brightly glowing cross

das ein Stück Natur alibihaft zurückholen will, sondern eine makellose Fläche aus dem Material der Wände, den Chromstahlplatten (hier allerdings ohne die Perforierungen), aus der sich plastikhaft eine freie Form erhebt, das Oberlicht, das auf die Lage des Altars weist, und eine am Rand der Fläche umlaufende Fuge, die an eine Art Reling erinnert.

Der Eingang in die Kirche liegt nicht direkt in der Blickachse des vom Bus- oder U-Bahnhof Kommenden, und er liegt auch nicht unterhalb des in die Wand eingelassenen großen, hellstrahlenden Kreuzes, was man vermuten könnte, sondern er liegt eher etwas beiseite, so, als wollte er jedes Repräsentieren von sich weisen, eben der Eingang in eine Kirche, der einlädt, und nicht das Portal, das eher abweist. Zwei Türflügel, mit hellem Metall belegt, bündig in die Wand eingelassen, daneben ein türhohes Fenster, davor ein schmales Podest, das die Schräge des rot asphaltierten Vorgeländes sichtbar macht und auf dem – wie ein sehr zurückhaltender Akzent – das offene U-förmige Profil, eine Art Zwischenraum, frei vor der Wand steht und dem Eingang Gewicht gibt, gefertigt aus Chromstahlplatten gleicher Art wie die Wand.

Aber es ist nicht nur das. Ein Wasserbecken, wie alles andere sehr zurückhaltend nicht über die Fläche der Quaderauskerbung hinausgehend, zieht den Blick weiter, um die Ecke herum auf eine zweite Doppeltür, auch mit hellem Metall belegt, auch bündig in der Wand liegend, aber doch sichtbar Nebeneingang, denn ein Podest oder ein Akzent betont diesen Eingang nicht; eine – mögliche – Öffnung, die den Kirchenraum mit dem Draußen verbinden kann, das hier zu einer Art Kirchenforum mit ansteigenden Sitzreihen gebildet ist und das trotz des pastosen und leeren Ambientes des Drumherum eine gewisse Intimität erreicht. Von hier führt ein kleiner Kirchweg am Läutewerk vorbei auf eine höher gelegene Wiese (fast ein Idyll im Meer der Härte) und um die Kirche herum zum Ausgangsort zurück. Und weiter führt von hier ein geschützt, geborgen, fast versteckt liegender Zugang in die Sakristei und in die Gemeinderäume hinein, die im Untergeschoß der Kirche liegen, taghell erleuchtet und sehr weiträumig disponiert; Räume, die man auch über einen tief gelegenen, stillen Gartenhof an der gegenüberliegenden Seite erreichen kann, dessen Brüstung, dessen Reling das Herauswachsen des Baukörpers aus dem Boden weiter sinnbildhaft verdeutlicht.

Zurück zum Eingang, zum Eingangsensemble, zum Weg in die Kirche hinein. Das, was also schon außen überrascht, dieses dunkel-violett Changierende, dieses Spiegelnde, dieses letztlich doch Helle trotz des vermeintlich Dunklen, das überrascht im Inneren mit – ja: barockem Effekt. Nach Öffnen der fensterlosen Metalltüren, nach Durchschreiten des Windfangs, der so kunstvoll gestaltet in das Gesamte integriert ist, der so hell und durchsichtig ist, daß das schnöde Wort »Windfang« eigentlich nicht passen will, nach diesen wenigen Schritten empfängt einen ein Raum, der den Atem für einen Moment stocken läßt, ein Raum von bewegender Schönheit: schön in den menschlichen Proportionen, schön in den Farben, hell und licht, schön – und raffiniert – in der Lichtführung, so daß man erst jetzt wirklich Tesars Wort »Naturlichtnotate« versteht.

Mit barockem Effekt: Peter Thumbs Wallfahrtskirche Birnau hoch über dem Bodensee steht als ein Beispiel, Dominikus Zimmermanns Wieskirche als ein anderes. Die Birnau: Der überwältigende Eindruck, wenn man, geblendet von der das Sonnenlicht zurückwerfenden Eingangsfassade, vom grellen Draußen die Kirche betritt, zunächst einen dunklen Korridor von geringer Raumhöhe passieren muß und erst dann in dem lichten, prachtvollen Innenraum steht, oder, stärker noch, der umgekehrte Weg, wenn man das Innere verläßt, wieder die dunkle Schleuse durchschreitet und dann das strahlende Panorama von Bodensee und gegenüberliegendem Höhenrücken und in der Ferne die Alpensilhouette vor Augen hat; vergleichbar hier in der Donau City das wenig menschlich aufgefaßte Vorfeld großspurig gegeneinander konkurrierender Massen, das einen sein Verlorensein empfinden läßt, dann dieser violett schimmernde, sich nach außen eher spröde gebende und dennoch anziehende Körper und dann dieser helle, warme, ja strahlende Raum, der einen schützend umfängt. Die Wieskirche: die Heiterkeit, die dieser schwingende Raum ausstrahlt und sich auf den Menschen überträgt, dieses so völlig Unpastose trotz des doch so überreichen Schmuckes, diese Klarheit des architektonischen Raumgedankens, der einen glauben lassen will, daß Architektur wie Musik sei, in dem man des Bauherrn Empfindung »hic loco habitat fortuna, hic quiescat cor« nachvollziehen kann; und ebenso empfinde ich es in Heinz Tesars Raum – hier wohnt das Glück, hier findet das Herz seine Ruhe.

In diesem Raum muß man verweilen, und man will es gern, in dieser bergenden Hülle, die durch ihre Proportionen und besonders durch das einheitliche Material für Wand, Boden, Decke und Gestühl, durch das helle Birkenholz ihre Ruhe aussendet und die durch die Lichtöffnungen lebt: die kleineren – diszipliniert verstreuten – kreisrunden, die großflächigen in den Einkerbungen, die das Licht, das Sonnenlicht einfangen und auf den Wänden wandern lassen, und die »Wunde« in der Decke, die Öffnung zum Zenit, die Licht auf den Altarstein fallen läßt.

Das Licht ist nicht starr, es lebt; es lebt durch das Wandern über die Wand, es lebt durch das Hereinholen der Alltagsbewegungen draußen durch die Rundfenster, und es lebt durch den Wechsel der Lichtintensität entsprechend dem Wechsel des Tageslichts. Man spürt das Lebendige, das, was man zum Beispiel in Egon Eiermanns Berliner Kaiser-Wilhelm-Gedächtniskirche nicht spürt und was diesen sonst so beeindruckenden Raum so eigentümlich starr macht: Zu welcher Tageszeit man das Innere auch betritt, morgens, mittags, nachts, ob bei Sonnenschein oder Regenwetter, immer ist der Eindruck der gleiche, eben starr, weil der Raum nicht natürlich, sondern künstlich beleuchtet wird, durch Strahler, die in dem rund 1,20 m breiten Umgang zwischen den beiden Wandscheiben, die den Raum umgeben, installiert sind und sowohl das Innere immer wie auch das Äußere bei Dunkelheit erleuchten lassen.

Man muß die sich mit dem Durchzug von Wolken vor der Sonne entsprechend schnell wandelnde Helligkeit in der Kathedrale von Chartres beobachtet haben – ein Ereignis von geradezu dramatischer Dimension; man muß den Wandel des Lichts in Franz Füegs Piuskirche in Meggen, diesem Quader, der rundum mit dünnen, durchscheinenden Marmorplatten gleichsam geschlossen und zugleich geöffnet ist, erlebt haben, oder eben in Tesars Raum, um den Unterschied ermessen zu können: dieses Gleiten vom Hellen zum Dunklen und umgekehrt, dieses gänzlich Anderswerden des Raumgefühls.

3. Egon Eiermann, Kaiser-Wilhelm-Gedächtniskirche, Berlin, 1957–63.
4. Franz Füeg, Piuskirche, Meggen bei Luzern, 1963.
5. Johann Lucas von Hildebrandt, Peterskirche, Wien, begonnen 1702.
6. Clemens Holzmeister, Maria Hilf, Bregenz-Vorkloster, 1924–31.

3. Egon Eiermann, Kaiser-Wilhelm-Gedächtniskirche, Berlin, 1957–63.
4. Franz Füeg, Piuskirche, Meggen near Lucerne, 1963.
5. Johann Lucas von Hildebrandt, Peterskirche, Vienna, begun in 1702.
6. Clemens Holzmeister, Maria Hilf, Bregenz-Vorkloster, 1924–31.

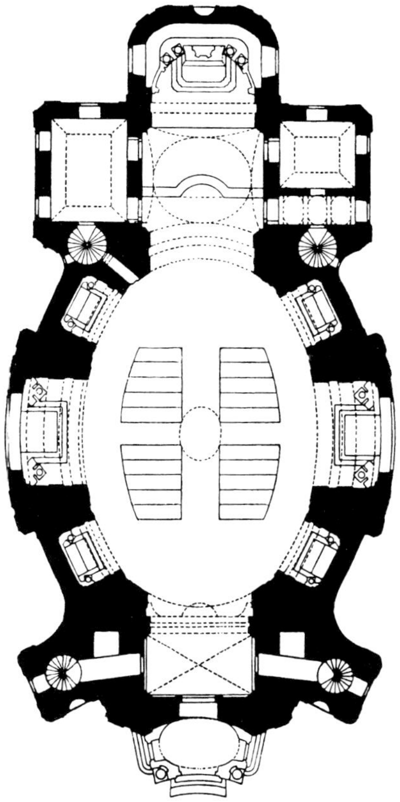

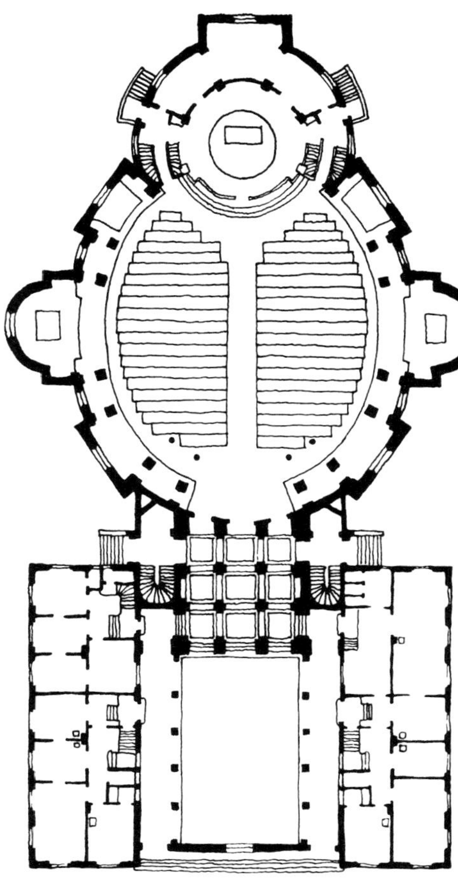

that is let into the wall, which one might anticipate. It is set a little to one side, as though wanting to efface itself from any sense of prestige. It is just the way into the church, it is inviting, it is not a portal, which tends to be forbidding. Two door leaves, with bright metal fittings, are set flush into the wall, and next to them is a window the same height as the door, with a small plinth in front of it that makes the slope on the red asphalt forecourt visible and on which – like a very reticent accent – the open U-shaped member stands, a kind of intermediate space, placed freely in front of the wall, lending weight to the entrance, and made of chromium steel sheets of the same kind as the wall.

But it is not just that. A pool of water, very reticent like everything else, as it does not exceed the area of the notch in the cuboid, takes our eyes further, round the corner to a second double door, also with light metal fittings, and also flush with the wall, but visibly a side entrance, as this entrance is not emphasized by a plinth or an accent; a – possible – opening that can link the church interior with the outside world. Here it makes a kind of church forum with rising rows of seats, achieving a kind of intimacy despite the turgid and empty ambience of everything around it. From here a little church paths leads past the bells to a lawn a little higher up (almost idyllic in the sea of hardness), round the church and back to the point at which it started. And there is also access from here, via a covered, secluded, almost hidden route, to the sacristy and the parish rooms in the basement of the church, lit as brightly as day and very spacious; rooms that can also be reached from a lower, quiet garden court on the opposite side, whose parapet, whose railing provides a further symbolic clarification of the way in which the building grows out of the ground.

Back to the entrance, to the entrance ensemble, to the way into the church. Something that is already surprising on the outside, this darkly purple iridescence, this mirror quality, this brightness despite the initial impression of darkness, that is an immediate surprise in the interior and makes an effect that is – yes: Baroque. After opening the windowless metal doors, after walking through the porch, which is so artfully built into the overall picture, which is so light and transparent that the mean little word porch hardly seems to fit, after these few steps we are greeted by a space that takes our breath away for a moment, a space that is movingly beautiful: beautiful in its human proportions, beautiful in its colours, light and bright, beautiful – and refined – in the handling of the light, so that it is now easy to understand Tesar's phrase »natural light notes«.

A Baroque effect: Peter Thumb's pilgrimage church in Birnau high above Lake Constance is one example, Dominikus Zimmermann's die Wies is another. Birnau: an overwhelming impression, when you come into the church, blinded by the sunlight reflected back from the entrance façade, from the harshly lit exterior. First you have to walk through a dark, low corridor, and only then are you in the light, magnificent interior, or, more strongly still, the opposite way, when you leave the interior, walk back through the dark lock and then see the gleaming panorama of Lake Constance with the mountain ridges opposite and in the distance the silhouette of the Alps; comparable here in the Donau City is the area in front of the church, which is not particularly human in its grandiose competing masses, as it makes the visitor feel lost, and then comes the violet shimmer of this body, which is essentially aloof and yet attractive on the outside, and then this warm, indeed radiant space that takes us in so protectively. The Wieskirche: the brightness that this swooping space radiates and then transfers to its visitors, this effect that is anything but turgid despite the enormously lavish ornament, this clarity of the overall architectural thinking, making you want to believe that architecture is like music, in which you can sense the feelings of the man who commissioned the church when he said »hic loco habitat fortuna, hic quiescat cor«; and that is exactly what I feel in Heinz Tesar's space – this is where happiness dwells, this is where the heart finds its peace.

You have to linger in this space, and you want to linger, in this soothing envelope that thrives on its proportions and especially on the uniform material for wall, floor, ceiling and pews, transmitting its stillness with the light birch-wood, drawing life from the apertures for light: the small ones scattered – but scattered with discipline – and circular, the large ones in the notches, which catch the light, the sunlight and let it wander over the walls, and the »wound« in the ceiling, the opening to the zenith, that allows light to fall on the altar-stone.

This light is not dead, it is alive; it is alive because it wanders across the walls, it is alive because the everyday movements from the outside world are brought inside by the round windows, and it is also alive because of the changing intensity of the light as the daylight changes. You have a sense of life, something that you do not have in Egon Eiermann's Kaiser-Wilhelm-Gedächtniskirche in Berlin, and that makes the otherwise extremely impressive space feel so strangely dead: it does not matter what time you come into the church, whether it is morning, noon or night, whether the sun is shining or it is raining, the impression is always the same: it is dead, and dead because the space is not lit naturally, but artificially, by floodlights installed in the ambulatory about 1.2 m wide between the two wall sections that surround the space, and that light the interior at all times, and make the exterior glow at night.

You need to have seen the rapidly changing brightness caused by clouds passing across the sun in Chartres cathedral – an event of almost dramatic dimensions, you have to have experienced the change in Franz Füeg's Piuskirche in Meggen, this cuboid that is closed, and at the same time opened, as it were, on all sides by thin, translucent marble slabs, or even in Tesar's space, in order to be able to assess the difference: this sliding from light to dark and back again, this way in which the feel of the space becomes completely different.

And so the space thrives on the way the light is handled, and it also thrives, as I have said, on its unity, in the light birch-wood that encloses everything; it thrives on the repose that it emanates, on the smoothness of the ceiling, broken only by the »light wound«, by the walls, rising without a base and equally without any sense of transition, on the benches arranged in a circle round the altar block; it thrives on the play of apertures, round and rectangular: the rectangular ones set in the wall flush and without reveals, different in size and arranged differently in relation to each other, the smaller and large round ones with deep, conical reveals, thrusting into the space in a sophisticated way, in various angular constellations, and it also thrives on the disruptions: the asymmetrical position of the altar in the space, the three differently sized segments of pews that

Der Raum lebt also durch die Lichtregie, und er lebt, wie gesagt, durch seine Einheitlichkeit, durch das allumfassende helle Birkenholz; er lebt durch die Ruhe, die er aussendet, durch die Glätte der Decke, die nur durch die »Lichtwunde« gebrochen ist, durch die sockellos aufsteigenden und ebenso übergangslos endenden Wände, durch die ringförmig um den Altarblock geordneten Bänke; er lebt durch das Spiel der Öffnungen, runder und rechteckiger – die rechteckigen, flächig und ohne Laibung in die Wand eingesetzt, unterschiedlich groß und unterschiedlich einander zugeordnet, die runden kleineren und größeren mit tiefer, konisch verlaufender Laibung, die unter verschiedenen Winkelkonstellationen differenziert in den Raum hineingreifen –, und er lebt durch die Störungen: die asymmetrische Lage des Altars im Raum, die drei verschieden großen Sitzbanksegmente, die ihn umschließen, die Position des vergoldeten Wandkreuzes, die der Zenit-Öffnung, die Lage der Eingangsinsel, und besonders die Einkerbungen der Quaderecken außen, die sich innen als Volumen abbilden. Diese Volumen sind auf der Altarseite schwebende Lichtkanzeln, spürbar Räume im Raum, ohne trennend zu sein, die Raumbereiche für den Taufstein und die Tabernakelstele mit dem ewigen Licht bilden und die auf der dem Altar abgewandten Seite scheinbare Eckpfeiler sind, durchlichtete Pfeiler, zwischen denen sich möbelartig und mit leichter Kurvierung ein Riegel mit dem herausgestellten Nebeneingang, dem Zugang zu den Gemeinderäumen im Untergeschoß, einem Beicht- und Aussprachezimmer sowie einem behindertengerechten Aufzug spannt und an deren einen sich der Windfang des Haupteingangs lehnt, oder, richtiger gesagt, mit ihm verschmilzt.

Mit diesen Störungen überspielt Tesar überzeugend das – im strengen Sinne – unlösbare Problem des reinen Zentralbaus, nämlich das Ideal, die Richtungslosigkeit mit der Zugänglichkeit in Einklang zu bringen, die eigentlich und rein theoretisch nur aus der Mitte heraus erfolgen dürfte, gleichsam dem Okulus des Pantheons in Rom entsprechend; oder, fast ebenso wirklichkeitsfremd, durch deckungsgleiche, symmetrisch liegende Eingänge an allen Seiten. Palladio hat einen solchen reinen Zentralbau verwirklichen können, seine Villa Rotonda am Stadtrand von Vicenza; aber diese Villa war quasi funktionslos, das heißt, sie diente nicht dem Wohnen, sondern sie diente der Repräsentation, sie war eine Art Baldachin für Festlichkeiten.

Aber der Zentralbau für die Kirche mit ihrer einer strengen Funktionalität unterworfenen Liturgie? Für Bramante war das Ideal des Zentralbaus ein Lebensthema, und mit seinem Tempietto in Rom ist ihm der reine Zentralbau – fast – gelungen; fast, weil er den Zugang zum eigentlichen Kultort im Untergeschoß beinahe kellertreppenartig irgendwo rückseitig versteckt. Mit seinem Projekt für den Neubau von St. Peter in Rom mußte er letztlich scheitern, weil sich die konsequente Regelmäßigkeit, weil sich vier gleichartige Portale an den Enden der Kreuzarme des Grundrisses (und der Altar richtungslos in der Mitte) nur schwer mit den Anforderungen der Kirche vereinbaren ließen. Und dennoch, trotz dieses grandiosen Scheiterns, dieses Scheiternmüssens, das ein warnendes Fanal hätte sein können, zieht sich der Wille zum Zentralbau durch die Architekturgeschichte besonders des Kirchenbaus hindurch, ungebrochen bis in die Gegenwart hinein.

Otto Bartning gelingt ein einheitlicher, wirklicher Zentralbau – in modernerer Zeit – vielleicht am ehesten mit seinem Sternkirchenprojekt von 1928 (das er dann später modifiziert in Essen verwirklichte), in dem er ein Segment des zentralen Raumes, eines weitgehend regelmäßigen Siebenecks mit gleichen Eingängen an sechs Seiten, aus dem Ganzen der »Predigtkirche« herausschneidet, als »Feierkirche«, als Raum im Raum, in eine erhöhte Ebene legt und damit die Richtungen auf den Altar hier, auf die Kanzel darunter dort mit der Richtungslosigkeit des Zentralraumes verschmelzen läßt.

Nach Bramante und seinen Nachfolgern, die nach dem – kaum erreichbaren – Ideal strebten (und in deren Tradition Bartnings Sternkirchenprojekt steht), suchte besonders das Zeitalter des Barocks den – praktikablen – Zentralbau und fand eine Lösung des Konflikts zwischen dem gewollten Zentralen und dem geforderten Gerichtetsein im Kompromiß des Überdeckens beider Forderungen, indem die reine, die regelmäßige Form in eine dynamische, indem die Kreisform des Grundrisses in ein Oval übergeführt, indem der Raum gestreckt und mit »kontrapunktischen« Gegenrichtungen ausgeglichen wird: Borromini in S. Carlo alle Quattro Fontane in Rom, Bernini in S. Andrea al Quirinale, Fischer von Erlach in Wien oder Salzburg, Hildebrandt im böhmischen Gabel, in Wien oder Linz, Christoph Dientzenhofer in Breunau und Smirschitz, Dominikus Zimmermann mit seiner Wieskirche oder in Steinhausen – Raumkonzepte, die ausstrahlen und weiterwirken und auf die in der neueren Architekturgeschichte etwa Clemens Holzmeister aufbaut mit seiner Kirche Maria Hilf in Bregenz-Vorkloster oder Dominikus Böhm mit seinem Projekt einer Meßopferkirche »Circumstantes« aus den frühen zwanziger Jahren, in deren Nachfolge vielleicht Rudolf Schwarz mit St. Michael in Frankfurt am Main oder der Theresienkirche in Linz steht.

Die große Mehrzahl der Architekten aber begegnet dem Grundproblem, das Zentrale mit dem Gerichteten zu verbinden, indem sie in das Gewollte, in das Ideal, das Geforderte mehr oder weniger gezwungen zu integrieren versucht: Michelangelo findet mit seinem mächtigen Portikus, den er, als eine Reaktion auf Bramante, vor den Zentralbau vor St. Peter legen will, ein Konzept, das wohl im römischen Pantheon einen seiner Ursprünge hat und das sich auswirkt über den Invalidendom in Paris, über Soufflots Panthéon, Weinbrenners katholische Stadtkirche in Karlsruhe und Schinkels Nikolaikirche in Potsdam bis hin in die Moderne, wiederum bis hin zu Holzmeister, zu seiner Pfarrkirche in Hamburg-Blankenese mit dem mächtigen Eingangsmassiv, das er vor die eigentliche Rotunde legt und das sein Pendant in einer Art Chor findet, ausgeglichen durch seitliche Öffnungen als eine Art Gegengewicht. Oder sich auswirkt bis zu Egon Eiermanns Berliner Kaiser-Wilhelm-Gedächtniskirche, dieses Oktogon mit nahezu deckungsgleichen Ansichten, das ein Gerichtetsein schon außen durch ein schweres, an Stahltrossen hängendes, tiefes Vordach geradezu demonstriert, eine Richtung, die innen durch die niedrige Raumhöhe unter der Orgelempore, durch die hoch aufragende Orgel selbst und durch den Altar weitergeführt wird und die das Zentrale weitgehend überdeckt; eine Richtung, der Eiermann gegenzusteuern versuchte durch eine Auflösung der Stuhlblöcke in verschiedene Einheiten (die nicht ausgeführt wurde) und durch ein filigranes Hängekreuz über dem Altar, das mit dem Raster der Wand zunächst verschmolz und erst auf den zweiten Blick sozusagen wirksam wurde, das Auge dadurch abgelenkt, der Eindruck des Gerichteten geschmälert war (bis eine

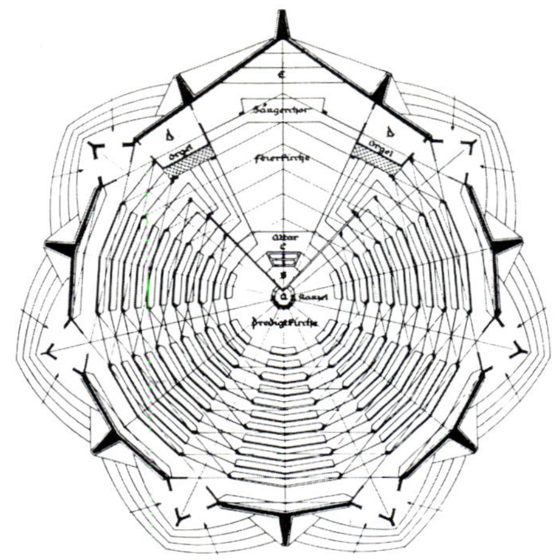

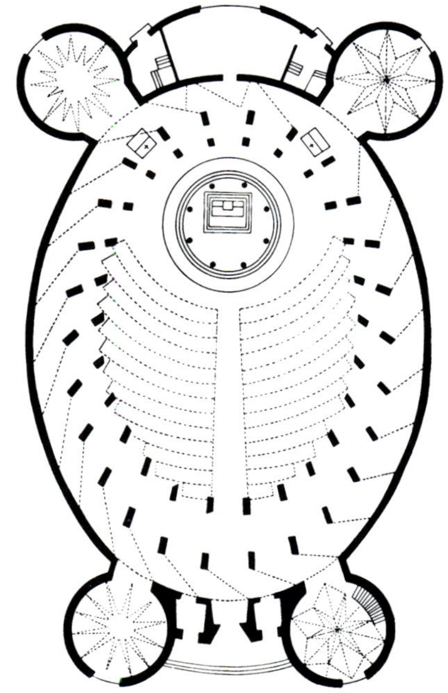

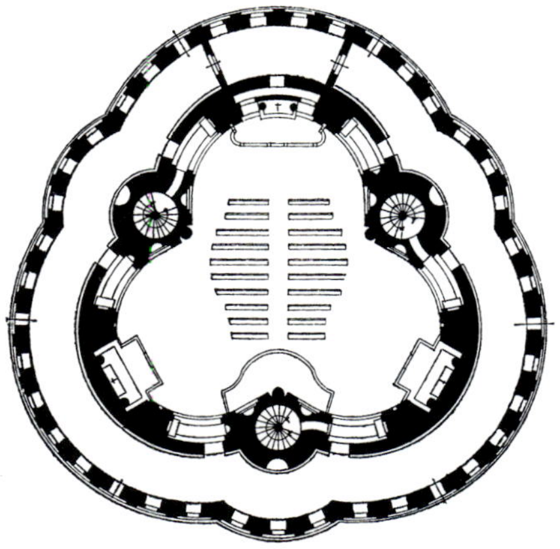

7. Otto Bartning, Sternkirche, 1922, Projekt.
8. Dominikus Böhm, »Circumstantes«, 1923, Projekt.
9. Georg Dientzenhofer, Dreifaltigkeitskapelle, Kappel bei Waldsassen, 1685–89.
10. Clemens Holzmeister, Maria Grün, Hamburg-Blankenese, 1929/30.
11. Rudolf Schwarz, St. Theresia, Linz, 1957–62.

7. Otto Bartning, Sternkirche, 1922, project.
8. Dominikus Böhm, »Circumstantes«, 1923, project.
9. Georg Dientzenhofer, Dreifaltigkeitskapelle, Kappel near Waldsassen, 1685–89.
10. Clemens Holzmeister, Maria Grün, Hamburg-Blankenese, 1929/30.
11. Rudolf Schwarz, St. Theresia, Linz, 1957–62.

surround it, the position of the gilded cross on the wall, the position of the zenith aperture, the placing of the entrance island and especially the inset corners of the cuboid, which create volumes in the interior. Volumes that are floating pulpits of light on the altar side, manifestly a space within the space, without creating a division, forming spaces for the font and the tabernacle column with the sanctuary lamp, and on the side that turns away from the altar they seem to form corner columns, transparent columns, and between them, like a piece of furniture, a slightly curved strip contains the exterior side entrance, access to the parish rooms on the basement floor, a room for confession and counselling and a lift suitable for the disabled, and against one of which the porch of the main entrance leans, or, to put it better, fuses together with it.

Tesar uses these disruptions as convincing cover for the – strictly speaking – insoluble problem of a pure centrally planned building, and that is the ideal of combining the lack of orientation with accessibility, which actually and purely theoretically ought to derive only from the centre, thus effectively taking a lead from the oculus of the Pantheon in Rom; or, and this is almost as incompatible with reality, by using identically, symmetrically arranged entrances on all sides. Palladio was able to realize a pure centrally planned building of this kind, his Villa Rotonda on the outskirts of Vicenza; but this villa was essentially devoid of function, in other words, no one lived in it, it was there for reasons of prestige alone, it was a kind of baldacchino for festivities.

But a central plan for a church, with its liturgy that is subject to the building's strong sense of function? For Bramante, the ideal of the centrally-planned building was a life-long theme, and he – almost – succeeded in creating a pure central plan with his Tempietto in Rome; almost, because he hid the entrance to the actual place of worship in the basement somewhere at the back, rather like a flight of cellar steps. His project for the new St. Peter's in Rome was ultimately doomed to fail, because it was difficult to reconcile the resultant regularity, the four identical portals at the ends of the arms of the cross on the ground plan (and the altar facing nowhere in the middle) with the requirements of a church. And nevertheless, despite this failure, this inevitable failure, which could have been a warning beacon, the desire to create centrally planned buildings runs right through the history of architecture, in an unbroken line to the present day.

Otto Bartning's 1928 Sternkirche (Star Church) project (which he later realized in Essen in modified form) perhaps came closest to a uniform, truly centrally planned building. Here he cuts a segment of the centrally planned space, a largely regular pentagon with identical entrances on six sides, out of the entirety of the »preaching church«, as a »celebratory church«, as a space within a space. He places this on a higher level, and thus fuses the orientation towards the altar here and the pulpit down below with the lack of orientation in the centrally planned space as a whole.

After Bramante and his successors, who were striving towards a – scarcely achievable – ideal (Bartning's Sternenkirche is in this tradition), the Baroque age in particular looked at the – practicable – centrally planned building and found a solution to the conflict between the desire for centrality and the sense of orientation that was required. They compromised by meeting both requirements: the pure, regular form is transposed into a dynamic one, the circular ground plan becomes an oval, the space is stretched and balanced with »contrapuntal« counter-orientations: Borromini's S. Carlo alle Quattro Fontane in Rome, Bernini's S. Andrea al Quirinale, Fischer von Erlach in Vienna or Salzburg, Hildebrandt in Gabel in Bohemia, in Vienna or Linz, Christoph Dientzenhofer in Breunau and Smirschitz, Dominikus Zimmermann with die Wies or in Steinhausen; these are radiant spatial concepts that live on, and that are being built on in recent architectural history by Clemens Holzmeister, for example, with his Maria Hilf church in Vorkloster, Bregenz, or Dominikus Böhm with this project for a »Circumstantes« church for the sacrifice of the mass in the early twenties, with the line perhaps continued by Rudolf Schwarz with St. Michael in Frankfurt am Main or the Theresienkirche in Linz.

But the majority of architects confronts the basic problem of combining centrally planned and oriented buildings by trying to integrate the wishes, the ideal, with more or less force into the requirements: Michelangelo's massive portico, which he intends to place in front of the centrally planned structure of St. Peter's as a response to Bramante, is a concept that probably originated in one sense from the Roman Pantheon, and that continues to make an effect on the dome of Les Invalides in Paris, on Soufflot's Panthéon, Weinbrenner's Katholische Stadtkirche in Karlsruhe and Schinkel's Nikolaikirche in Potsdam, then right down to Modernism, and on to Holzmeiser, with his parish church in Blankenese, Hamburg, with the powerful entrance massif that he places in front of the actual rotunda. with its counterpart in a kind of choir, balanced by side apertures as counterweights of a sort; it also affected Eiermann's Kaiser-Wilhelm-Gedächtniskirche in Berlin, that octagon with almost identical aspects that practically insists upon a sense of orientation even on the outside with the deep, heavy canopy suspended on steel hawsers, an orientation that is continued in the interior by the low space under the organ loft, the towering organ itself and the altar, and all this largely conceals the central plan; an orientation that Eiermann tries to counter by dissolving the blocks of pews into different units (something that was not done) and by suspending a filigree cross above the altar that first of all blended into the grid of the wall and only became effective at a second glance, so to speak, the eye diverted by it, reducing the impression of orientation (until an illuminated golden figure of Christ replaced the cross and destroyed the subtle network of forces by making an unduly eye-catching statement).

Georg Dientzenhofer makes it almost impossible to detect orientation towards a high altar in his planning concept for the Dreifaltigkeitskirche in Kappel near Waldsassen, by almost hiding it in regular trefoil archictecture: in the church of Santa Maria della Salute in Venice, Baldassare Longhena has the main portal disappear within the backdrop of the overall forms, and from close up and at a distance largely forces the choir out of the centre of attention. He does not emphasize it in the interior either, so that the space works as it is intended to work: it looks centrally planned; Georg Bähr reacts comparably in Dresden (the choir of his Frauenkirche plays a largely subordinate role, inside and out), and Dominikus Böhm is comparable – to an extent – with his church of St. Engelbert in Riehl, Cologne, this »lemon-squeezer« that radiates both repose and dynamism, has internal orientation that one would be very

angestrahlte goldene Christusfigur anstelle des Kreuzes mit allzu plakativer Aussage das feine Kräftegeflecht zerstörte).

Georg Dientzenhofer läßt in seinem Planungskonzept der Dreifaltigkeitskirche in Kappel bei Waldsassen die Ausrichtung auf einen Hauptaltar kaum erkennen, versteckt sie quasi in der regelmäßigen Dreipaßarchitektur. Baldassare Longhena läßt in der Kirche S. Maria della Salute in Venedig außen das Hauptportal im Gros der kulissenartigen Formen verschwinden und drängt den Chor aus der Nah- und Fernsicht weitgehend ins Abseits, läßt ihn im Inneren unbetont, so daß der Raum so wirkt, wie er wirken sollte: als Zentralraum. Georg Bähr reagiert in Dresden vergleichbar (der Chor seiner Frauenkirche spielt außen wie innen eine weitgehend untergeordnete Rolle), und ebenso – in Ansätzen – vergleichbar ist Dominikus Böhm mit seiner Kirche St. Engelbert in Köln-Riehl, diese ebenso Ruhe wie Dynamik ausstrahlende »Zitronenpresse«, deren innere Richtung, gegeben durch eine Freitreppe und durch ein wie angeheftet wirkendes Chorgehäuse, man gern übersehen würde. Und Auguste Perret schließlich läßt in seiner Kathedrale Saint-Joseph für das aus den Kriegszerstörungen wiedererstehende Le Havre (fast kontrapunktisch zu Tesars Architekturauffassung) den über 90 m hoch aufragenden Schlot auf einer Art würfelförmigem Sockel als Krone des Altars – und als Krone der Stadt – in einem gerichteten Unterbau mühsam und gestalterisch wenig überzeugend versinken.

Und Tesar selbst? Er formt auch den Zentralbau, versieht ihn aber, wie gesagt, mit den sensiblen Störungen, so daß sich das Zentrale mit der notwendigen Ausrichtung auf den Altar, mit der Blickachse Eingang – Altarblock – Wandkreuz, die »über Eck« geführt und nicht gradlinig ist, so daß sich also das Zentrale mit dem Gerichteten auf ungekünstelte Art verbindet. Ein Raum mit großem Atem, in dem der Altarblock, der dunkle Monolith, wie selbstverständlich und nicht als Zutat steht (und in den kaum sichtbar und sehr zurückhaltend die Reliquie eingefügt ist), indirekt gehöht durch die Lichtöffnung zum Zenit und durch das schlichte Kreuz, das unaufdringlich und von starker Wirkung mit einem kreisrunden, nur schimmernden Plafond bündig in die Wand eingelassen ist, eben jenem Plafond, der sich außen durch einen Bezirk ohne Lichtöffnungen in der Wand abzeichnet, und gleichermaßen selbstverständlich stehen der Ambo, der Taufstein, die Tabernakelstele und anderes liturgisches Gerät, ohne jede Unproportionalität von Gefühl und Form.

Ist dieser Bau, ist dieser Raum sakral? Ist Mies van der Rohes Chicagoer Studentenkapelle sakral, dieser kastenförmige Bau, der sich mit seiner großen, nüchtern gestalteten Glaswand nach außen öffnet und an dem außer einem verchromten und schon von weitem sichtbaren Kreuz über dem Altar nichts auf den geistigen Inhalt dieses Hauses hinweist, ein Bau, der ebenso ein Haus Gottes sein könnte wie auch ein Haus der Technik? Ist Eiermanns Berliner Kaiser-Wilhelm-Gedächtniskirche sakral, in der den Besucher ein geradezu mystisches tiefblaues Dunkel empfängt, gänzlich introvertiert, ohne jeden Blickkontakt nach außen, mit einigen Glanzlichtern, die sich dem Auge nur zögernd offenbarten (ursprünglich, vor der Hängung der heute den Gesamteindruck verunklärenden grellen Christusfigur)? Ist Rudolf Schwarz' Aachener Fronleichnamskirche sakral, dieser außen strahlend weiße, innen schwarzweiße Kubus, dessen konzentrierte Kargheit und Schmucklosigkeit scheinbar so gar nichts Kirchliches hat? Ist Gottfried Böhms Wallfahrtskirche in Neviges, die an eine imposante Gralsburg denken läßt, für deren Inneres alle Register der Stimmungsarchitektur gezogen sind und die sich dem Gefühl des Besuchers auch unmittelbar mitteilt, sakral? Ist es Le Corbusiers amorphe Höhle in Ronchamp mit ihren dramatisch-gegensätzlichen Lichteffekten oder Fritz Högers Berliner Kirche am Hohenzollernplatz in ihrem Widerspruch von Innen und Außen, in ihrem »Himmelsstrebenden«, ihrer Ausstrahlung von »Sehnsucht und Mystik, wie sie in gotischen Domen nicht größer sein kann«, wie Höger zu seinem Bau schreibt, in »ihrer Lichtfülle aus unsichtbarer Quelle – im wahrsten Sinne Mystik des Lichts« ?

Ist Franz Füegs Meggener Kirche sakral, diese in ihrer großen Form einfache und im Einzelnen streng gegliederte Halle, in deren Innerem den Besucher ein wohliges, durch die dünnen Marmorwände warm gedämpftes Licht umfängt, oder Eiermanns Pforzheimer Matthäuskirche, die aus vergleichbarem architektonischen Wollen entstanden ist und für die es der Architekt nicht mit Kirchlichkeit oder kirchlichem Fühlen als unvereinbar ansah, das Altarpodium sichtbar mit reiner Haustechnik, nämlich mit den Austrittsöffnungen für die Warmluftheizung, zu verbinden und in den Turm die Abgas-Züge zu integrieren? Ist Otto Wagners Kirche am Steinhof in Wien sakral, für deren Innenraum, den Forderungen an eine Heil- und Pflegeanstaltskirche entsprechend, das Hygienische ein nicht unwesentliches Moment der architektonischen Gestaltung war, von der Technik der Weihwasserspender bis hin zu den Kacheln an den Wänden und auf dem Boden? Ist schließlich Heinz Tesars Bau sakral, hinter dessen Blockhaftigkeit, fehlte das signifikante Kreuz, man nicht unbedingt eine Kirche vermuten müßte; ist es der lichte, unpathetische Innenraum von saalartiger Weite und Offenheit?

Otto Bartning hat einmal gesagt: »Wenn wir ein Gemeindehaus bauen, wissen wir, was wir wollen, wenn wir eine Kirche bauen, wissen wir es nicht« – eine Unsicherheit, die zu den zahllosen gedanklich wie gestalterisch überfrachteten Kirchenbauten geführt hat, deren gewolltes inneres Wesen sich dem Gläubigen aber nicht mitteilt, es sei denn, er hätte ein Buch der Interpretation ständig zur Hand. Was den Menschen früher sakral gewesen ist, glauben wir heute in historischen Kirchen, in den romanischen, gotischen und barocken Bauten besonders, nachempfinden zu können. Was heute sakral sein könnte, läßt sich – vielleicht – mit Worten umschreiben, aber kaum auf eine präzise Formel bringen, und erst recht läßt sich dieses Sakrale nicht gezielt erzwingen. Sakralität steht nicht im Ermessen von Bauherren und Architekten, sondern das Sakrale kann sich unerwartet und ungewollt einfinden, oder es findet sich nicht ein. Es stellt sich also die Frage, ob man überhaupt eine Kirche unter der Prämisse, Sakralität erreichen zu wollen, bauen kann. Ob man diese Frage bejaht oder verneint – es bleibt die Notwendigkeit, den Gemeinden für den Gottesdienst einen schützenden Raum zu geben, mithin einen Zweckbau zu bilden, der höchsten übergeordneten Zwecken zu dienen hat. Oder, anders gesagt: Es wäre dem Kirchenbau heute durchaus angemessen, wenn man an ihn keine sakrale Forderung, sondern höchstens eine sakrale Erwartung stellen würde, von der man hofft, daß sie sich erfüllt.

»Von den gewaltigen Kirchenbauten der Vergangenheit«, schreibt in diesem Sinne Karl Scheffler in seinem Buch *Moderne Baukunst* aus dem Jahr 1908, und ich

12. Dominikus Böhm, St. Engelbert, Köln, 1930–32.
13. Auguste Perret, Saint-Joseph, Le Havre, 1951–56.
14. Ludwig Mies van der Rohe, Kapelle des Illinois Institute of Technology, Chicago, 1949–52.
15. Gottfried Böhm, Wallfahrtskirche in Velbert-Neviges, 1962 bis 1964.
16. Egon Eiermann, Matthäuskirche, Pforzheim, 1952/53.
17. Fritz Höger, Kirche am Hohenzollernplatz, Berlin, 1930 bis 1933.

12. Dominikus Böhm, St. Engelbert, Cologne, 1930–32.
13. Auguste Perret, Saint-Joseph, Le Havre, 1951–56.
14. Ludwig Mies van der Rohe, chapel of the Illinois Institute of Technology, Chicago, 1949–52.
15. Gottfried Böhm, pilgrimage church in Velbert-Neviges, 1962–64.
16. Egon Eiermann, Matthäuskirche, Pforzheim, 1952/53.
17. Fritz Höger, church in Hohenzollernplatz, Berlin, 1930 to 1933.

happy to overlook, derived as it is from an open staircase and a housing for the choir that looks as though is has been stapled on. And finally Auguste Perret, in his St. Joseph's Cathedral for Le Havre, rising out of the ruins of war damage (almost in counterpoint to Tesar's view of architecture), allows the chimney-like spire, over 90 m high, towering over a kind of cubic plinth as the crown of the altar – and of the town – to sink laboriously into an oriented sub-structure that is not at all convincing as a design.

And Tesar himself? He also follows a central plan, but provides it, as I have said, with sensitive disruptions, so that the centrally planned element links up with the necessary orientations to the altar, with the sight-line formed by entrance – altar block – wall cross, which runs »across the corner« and not in a straight line, so that the centrally planned element is combined with the oriented element in a completely natural way. A space on a grand scale, then, in which the altar block, the dark monolith, looks as though it is intended to be there, and not like an afterthought (and the reliquary is fitted into it almost invisibly and very reticently as well), raised indirectly by the zenith light aperture and by the plain cross, set unassertively flush into the wall and making a powerful effect with a circular and merely shimmering ceiling, the very ceiling that can be seen from the outside as an area without lighting apertures in the wall. The ambo, the font, the tabernacle column and other liturgical features are placed just as naturally, without any disproportion in terms of feeling or form.

Is this a religious building, is it a religious space? Is Mies van der Rohe's student chapel in Chicago religious, this box-shaped building opening up to the outside world with its large, austerely designed glass wall, with nothing about it to indicate its spiritual significance other than a chromium-plated cross on the altar that is visible from some distance, a structure that could just as much be a house of God as a house of technology? Is Eiermann's Kaiser-Wilhelm-Gedächtniskirche in Berlin religious, where visitors are received in an almost mystical, profoundly blue darkness, entirely introverted without any sight of the outside world, with its own highlights that revealed themselves to visitors only reluctantly (originally, before the introduction of the garish suspended figure of Christ, which now blurs the overall impression)? Is Rudolf Schwarz's Fronleichnamskirche in Aachen religious, this cube that is gleaming white on the outside and black-white on the inside, whose concentrated bleakness and lack of decoration seem to have nothing church-like about them? Is Gottfried Böhm's pilgrimage church in Neviges religious, reminiscent as it is of an imposing castle of the grail, with its interior pulling out all the atmospheric architectural stops and also playing directly on the visitor's emotions; is Le Corbusier's amorphous cave in Ronchamp religious, with its dramatic contrasting light effects or Fritz Höger's Berlin church in Hohenzollernplatz with its contradictions between interior and exterior, in its »striving towards heaven«, its radiation of »longing and mysticism, which could not be any greater in Gothic cathedrals«, as Höger wrote about his building, in »its abundance of light from an invisible source – in the truest sense the mysticism of light«?

Is Franz Füegg's church in Meggen religious, the hall that is simple in its greater form and austerely articulated in detail, in whose interior the visitor is welcomed by an agreeable light, warmly muted by the thin marble walls, of Eiermanns Matthäuskirche in Pforzheim, which was produced by a comparable architectural will, and in which the architect did not feel it incompatible with an ecclesiastical quality or ecclesiastical feeling to combine the altar podium visibly with pure building service technology, in other words the vents for the warm air heating, and to build the exhaust flues into the tower? Is Otto Wagner's Kirche am Steinhof in Vienna religious, in whose interior, appropriately for the demands of a mental home, hygiene was a crucial element of the architectural design, from the technology of the stoup to the tiles on the walls and the floor? And finally, is Tesar's building religious: one might not necessarily imagine there to be a church behind its block-like form, were it not for the significant cross; and is the light, unemotional interior with its hall-like width and openness religious?

Otto Bartning once said: »When we build a parish hall we know what we want, when we build a church we don't« – an uncertainty that has led to countless church buildings that are overloaded both intellectually and in terms of design, but their intended inner essence does not convey itself to the worshippers, unless they constantly have a book in their hands to interpret it for them. Nowadays we think we can find what people used to see as religious in historical churches, particularly in Romanesque, Gothic and Baroque buildings. It is – perhaps – possible to define what could be seen as religious today in words, but it could scarcely be reduced to a precise formula, and this religious quality can certainly not be forced into existence. A religious quality cannot be gauged or measured by clients and architects, but it can appear unexpectedly and unintentionally, or it might not appear at all. And so the question arises of whether it is at all possible to build a church under the premise of wanting to achieve a religious quality. Whether the answer to this question is yes or no – the necessity remains to provide congregations with a protective space for their services, and thus to create a functional building that has to fulfil the highest of higher functions; or put in another way: it would be entirely appropriate for church buildings today if one were not to demand that they should be religious, but simply to expect it of them, and then to hope that this expectation is fulfilled.

»When faced with the mighty churches of the past«, writes Karl Scheffler on this subject in his 1908 book *Moderne Baukunst*, and I think that his ideas have lost nothing of their topicality today, »When faced with the churches of the past, where we enjoy a compelling sense of worship amidst their visible beauty, ... we tend to forget the functionally empirical and indeed austere thinking that shaped these buildings. And the intellectual Romantics of our day think that this ›frozen music‹ could only be created in the way that he probably imagines the origins of the ›Ninth Symphony‹: in a sacred exuberance of emotion, through the inspired genius of a divinely gifted personality ... But the individual master builders did not behave ... in any way differently from an architect today when asked to build department stores. The ecclesiastical master builders of the Middle Ages created forms just as rationally, as demanded by the rites, as their successors today meet an essentially secular need.«

To return to Otto Bartning's formulation, when we build a parish hall we know what we want, when we build a church we don't. I think that Heinz Tesar knew – in this sense – what he wanted; he set himself to serve

meine, daß seine Gedanken bis heute nichts an Aktualität verloren haben, »von den Kirchenbauten der Vergangenheit, wo wir mit der sichtbaren Schönheit die bezwingende Kultstimmung genießen, ... vergessen wir leicht, welch sachlich empirischer, ja nüchterner Sinn diese Gebäude gebildet hat. Dem intellektuellen Romantiker der Gegenwart ist es, als könne diese ›gefrorene Musik‹ nur so geschaffen worden sein, wie er sich etwa die Entstehung der ›Neunten Symphonie‹ denkt: im heiligen Überschwang des Gefühls, durch die geniale Inspiration einer begnadeten Individualität. ... Die einzelnen Baumeister aber haben sich ... nicht im geringsten anders verhalten, wie es ein Architekt heute tut, wenn er Warenhäuser zu bauen hat. Genauso rationell, wie dieser ein vorwiegend profanes Bedürfnis einkleidet, haben die Kirchenbaumeister des Mittelalters Formen geschaffen, wie sie vom Ritus verlangt wurden.«

Noch einmal Otto Bartnings Wort: Wenn wir ein Gemeindehaus bauen, wissen wir, was wir wollen, wenn wir eine Kirche bauen, wissen wir es nicht. Ich meine, Heinz Tesar wußte – in diesem Sinne zu verstehen –, was er wollte; er hat sich in den Dienst der Bescheidenheit im Überfluß gestellt, und es ist ihm ein Bauwerk gelungen jenseits von intellektueller Romantik, »rationell, wie es der Ritus verlangt«, in dem sich der Atem des Sakralen einstellt – ich jedenfalls habe es so empfunden, wie ich es vorher vergleichbar nur in Heinrich Tessenows Berliner Ehrenmal Unter den Linden empfunden habe (trotz der nachträglich dorthinein plazierten aufgeblasenen Figur anstelle des ursprünglich hier stehenden einfachen, übermannshohen Monolithen mit dem stilisierten Kranz darauf), in diesem in seiner Schlichtheit ergreifend schönen Raum, von oben belichtet und ohne ein Zuviel an Gegenständen, der mit Schinkels verbliebener Raumhülle der Neuen Wache zusammengeht, als sei es immer so gewesen, und für den mehr als sonst Winckelmanns Wort von der edlen Einfalt und stillen Größe gilt.

Tesar ist – aus meiner Sicht – ein Raum gelungen, in dem sich der Atem des Sakralen einstellt, und es ist ihm, so sehe ich es jedenfalls, nicht nur hier gelungen: das Sakrale, das empfunden werden mag aus einer Steigerung des Gefühls, des seelischen Erlebens, ausgelöst durch eine besondere Raum- und Lichtregie, einen gezielten Kontrast von Außen und Innen, durch das Überraschungsmoment, durch die bewußte Inszenierung von Raumfolgen, inszeniert für den, der diese Räume in lebendigen Gebrauch nimmt: für den Menschen; und das – ich wiederhole es – in fast barocker Dimension, über die Tesars Kirche (nicht nur, aber für mich nachhaltig spürbar) in die Tradition und auch in sein eigenes Werk, zumindest Teile seines Werkes, eingebunden ist.

Das Schömerhaus in Klosterneuburg, eigentlich doch ein Haus für die eher nüchternen Belange der Verwaltung eines Konzerns, dessen Ansichten durch ihre Plastizität, durch die Ausbuchtungen, die Differenzierung des Materials zwar schon etwas anderes als das Gewohnte erahnen lassen, in dessen Innerem man aber kaum eine solch lichtdurchflutete, weite, ovale Rotunde erwartet hätte (eine Grundrißdisposition, die im Gesamten an Schinkels Altes Museum am Berliner Lustgarten erinnert), mit einem Treppenhaus darin, das wirklich wie ein Haus im Haus in den Raum hineingestellt ist, eine Plastik, in die man hineingehen kann; ein Raum, der gleichermaßen an Frank Lloyd Wrights New Yorker Guggenheim-Museum erinnert wie an Otto Wagners feingliedrige Architektur oder auch – entfernter – an die »Überraschungsarchitektur« Fischer von Erlachs, seine Wiener Karlskirche zum Beispiel, hinter deren ausponderierter »Versatzstückfassade« man auch nicht unbedingt einen längsovalen Fast-Zentralbau vermuten müßte.

Auch Tesars Ausstellungsgebäude für die Sammlung Essl in Klosterneuburg lebt aus diesen Momenten: das karge, elegant-karge Äußere, das auch einen Industriebau mit Würde vertreten könnte, der versteckte Zugang dort, wo man ihn nicht gleich vermutet, und dann im Inneren diese sich steigernde Folge unterschiedlichster Raumfigurationen bis hin zum großen – ja sakralen – Ausstellungssaal unter der sich in weitem Bogen auf- und niedersenkenden Decke.

Oder der Entwurf für eine Synagoge in Dresden, ein sich geradezu dramatisch aufbäumender, im Grundriß quadratischer und sehr hoher Raum, der durch seine ungewohnte Form und durch eine magische Lichtaussage seinem inneren Wesen entsprechend hätte wirken sollen; der Zugang erst im Obergeschoß nach Abschreiten eines bewußt geführten Weges, das Eintreten in der Diagonalen – wiederum der inszenierte Raum in barocker Dimension.

Oder Tesars kleine evangelische Kirche in Klosterneuburg, ein geschwungener Baukörper, der zunächst nicht unbedingt an eine Kirche denken ließe, wenn nicht das freistehende Kreuz davor ein entsprechendes Signal gäbe, der sich dem Ankommenden fast schutzschildartig entgegenstellt und erst im Umschreiten seine bewegten Konturen und sein eigentliches Gesicht freigibt und dann im Inneren einen wirklich barocken Raum

18. Heinz Tesar, Schömerhaus, Klosterneuburg, 1985 bis 1987.
19. Heinz Tesar, Sammlung Essl, Klosterneuburg, 1996 bis 1999.
20. Heinz Tesar, evangelische Kirche in Klosterneuburg, 1993–95.
21. Heinz Tesar, Synagoge in Dresden, 1997, Projekt.
22, 23. Johann Bernhard Fischer von Erlach, Karlskirche, Wien, begonnen 1716.

18. Heinz Tesar, Schömerhaus, Klosterneuburg, 1985 to 1987.
19. Heinz Tesar, Sammlung Essl, Klosterneuburg, 1996 to 1999.
20. Heinz Tesar, Prostestant church in Klosterneuburg, 1993–95.
21. Heinz Tesar, synagogue in Dresden, 1997, project.
22, 23. Johann Bernhard Fischer von Erlach, Karlskirche, Vienna, begun in 1716.

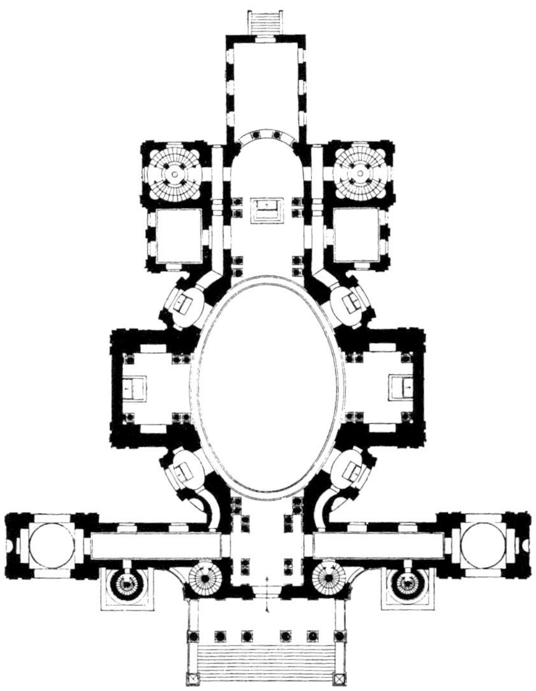

modesty in superfluity, and he has succeeded in creating a building that lies beyond intellectual romanticism, »rationally, as demanded by the rites«, in which the breath of religion can be felt – in any case that is the impression it made on me, something I have known in a comparable way before only in Heinrich Tessenow's monument in Unter den Linden in Berlin (despite the inflated figure that has been placed in there subsequently instead of the simple monolith a little higher than a man, with stylized wreath on top), in this space that is so movingly beautiful in its simplicity, lit from above and not cluttered with objects, fitting in with Schinkel's spatial envelope of the Neue Wache as though it had always been like this, and deserving Winckelmann's formulation about noble simplicity and quiet greatness more than most things do.

Tesar has succeeded – in my view – in creating a space in which the breath of religion can be felt, and, also as I see it, he has not only succeeded here: a religious sense, which may be felt as a result of the heightening of emotion, of spiritual experience, triggered by a particular treatment of space and light, a deliberate contrast between exterior and interior, by the element of surprise, by the conscious manipulation of spatial sequences, manipulated for the benefit of those who make living use of these spaces: for human beings; and all this – I repeat – on an almost Baroque scale, through which Tesar's church (not only, but in a way that I am lastingly aware of) is tied into tradition and also into his own work, or at least into parts of his work.

The Schömerhaus in Klosterneuburg was actually built to meet the requirements of running a group of companies, and its appearance certainly suggests something less than usual in its sculptural quality, in the protrusions, the differentiation of materials. But you would never have expected such a broad, oval rotunda in the interior, such a flood of light (the arrangement of the ground plan is reminiscent overall of Schinkel's Altes Museum by the Lustgarten in Berlin), with a staircase that really is placed in the space like a building within a building, a sculpture that you can walk into; a space that is as reminiscent of Frank Lloyd Wright's Guggenheim Museum in New York as it is of Otto Wagner's delicate architecture, or also – more distantly – of Fischer von Erlach's »surprise architecture«, his Karlskirche in Vienna, for example, behind the balanced masses of whose »set-piece façade« you would also not necessarily feel inclined to anticipate an oval almost-centrally-planned building.

And Tesar's exhibition building for the Essl Collection in Klosterneuburg also draws its life from these elements: the stark, elegantly stark exterior, that could also hold up its head with dignity as an industrial building, the hidden point of access where you are least expecting it, and then inside this sequence, stepping itself up gradually, of an enormous range of spatial configurations, culminating in the large – indeed: religious – exhibition hall under the ceiling that rises and falls in a wide arc.

Or the design for a synagogue in Dresden, a very high space on a square ground plan that rears up almost dramatically, intended to make its effect through its unusual form and through a magical light statement appropriate to its inner nature; access is only in the upper storey, after visitors have passed along a deliberately controlled route, walking in on the diagonal – once again, space manipulated on a Baroque scale.

Or Tesar's little Protestant church in Klosterneuburg, a curved building that would not make you think it was a church straight away if it were not for the appropriate signal from the free-standing cross in front of the building, which confronts visitors almost like a protective shield. It is only when walking round it that its mobile contours and its actual face are revealed, and then in the interior we find a truly Baroque space for the 20th century: on an oval ground plan with a curved ceiling and countless window apertures, apparently distributed at random over the whole space, even the ceiling, apertures that cast a picturesque light over the closed wall surfaces – a building that is self-confident in its modesty. And finally, to return to the starting-point again, the »Baroque spirit« of the church in the Donau City.

But of course it is not just the Baroque scale, the Baroque tradition that was almost bound to be an influence in the Vienna of Fischer von Erlach and Hildebrandt: the Karlskirche with its deliberate dissonances, its almost post-Modern assembly of various set-pieces from the type case of past building history to produce harmonious unity; the routes to be followed, the intensification of the space in the Upper Belvedere; the spatial fusion in the Hofbibliothek, the rhythm that gives this spatial sequence its internal size and that is announced almost imperceptibly in the view from the Hof side; the power of the interior and exterior space of the Peterskirche, the balanced proportions – what real architect could walk past that without being impressed.

And so it is not just the Baroque tradition in which I see Tesar and his church in the Donau City rooted; it is, starting off from here, the tradition of Modernism. There is a path that leads from Fischer von Erlach's dissonant Karlskirche, where history reveals itself as the present, to Jǒse Plečnik, of whom I was spontaneously reminded when I started working on Tesar's buildings, his way of creating unmistakable situations and making free use of the historical background as a stimulus and not as a collection of forms, his way of making architecture »as an expression of his person and as a directly comprehensible amalgam, difficult to trace back to its elements, of the contemporary and the traditional, of modern and historical memory«, as it said in 1986 in a Bauwelt article on Plečnik's work, architecture, coming back to Tesar, that is not, as he – Tesar – says, simply a way of meeting needs. He goes on to say that as an architect one should not commit oneself to fulfilling any programme without thinking, and to this extent one needs a private approach, to get to the bottom of things, and also an approach that is distanced and critical. One's own opinion has to be built into the work.

There are common features, affinities both overall and in detail: Plečnik's Church of the Sacred Heart in Prague, as highly individual as it is impressive, its surprising interiors (the austerely articulated main space, wide as a hall, making an almost classical statement, the barrel-vaulted, essentially squat lower church, reminiscent of revolutionary architecture, of Boullée, of Gilly or of early Weinbrenner, the high, brightly-lit ramped space in the tower massif), the design of the outside walls with their inclusions (or that of the National and University Library in Ljubljana) – the approaches are comparable: Tesar's large-scale form, as seen in the church in Klosterneuburg, the Dresden synagogue project or the church in the Donau City, its unmistakable interiors, the treatment of the wall surfaces, the notching on the Schömerhaus façade, the apertures in the

des 20. Jahrhunderts auftut: auf ovalem Grundriß, mit geschwungener Decke und unzähligen Fensteröffnungen, scheinbar unregelmäßig über den ganzen Raum, auch über die Decke, verteilt, Öffnungen, die ein malerisches Lichtbild auf die geschlossenen Wandflächen werfen – ein Bau von selbstbewußter Bescheidenheit. Und schließlich, um wieder an den Ausgangspunkt zurückzukehren, der »barocke Geist« der Kirche in der Donau City.

Aber es ist – natürlich – nicht nur die barocke Dimension, die barocke Tradition, die im Wien Fischer von Erlachs und Hildebrandts fast zwangsläufig von Einfluß ist: die Karlskirche mit ihren gewollten Dissonanzen, ihrer geradezu postmodernen Zusammenstellung verschiedener Versatzstücke aus dem Setzkasten vergangener Baugeschichte zu einer harmonischen Einheit; die Wegeführung, die Raumsteigerungen im Oberen Belvedere; die Raumverschmelzung in der Hofbibliothek, der Rhythmus, der dieser Raumfolge ihre innere Größe gibt und der sich schon außen in der Hofansicht kaum merklich ankündigt; die innen- und außenräumliche Kraft der Peterskirche, die Ausgewogenheit der Proportionen – welcher wirkliche Architekt könnte daran unbeeindruckt vorübergehen.

Es ist also nicht nur die barocke Tradition, in der ich Tesar, seine Kirche in der Donau City verwurzelt sehe; es ist, von hier den Weg einschlagend, die Tradition der Moderne. Von Fischer von Erlachs dissonanter Karlskirche, an der sich Geschichte als Gegenwart zeigt, führt ein Weg zu Jože Plečnik, an den ich spontan, als ich mich mit Tesars Bauten befaßte, erinnert war, seine Art, unverwechselbare Situationen herauszubilden und den geschichtlichen Hintergrund als Anregung und nicht als Formensammlung zum freien Gebrauch zu begreifen, seine Art, eine Architektur zu bilden »als Ausdruck seiner Person und als unmittelbar einleuchtendes, schwer auf seine Elemente zurückzuführendes Amalgam von Gegenwärtigem und Überkommenem, von moderner und historischer Erinnerung«, wie es 1986 in einem *Bauwelt*-Beitrag zu Plečniks Werk hieß, eine Architektur, auf Tesar bezogen, die nicht, wie er – Tesar – sagt, einfach nur Bedarfsdeckung sei. Denn als Architekt dürfe man sich nicht dazu hergeben, gedankenlos irgendwelche Programme zu erfüllen, und insofern brauche man einen privaten Ansatz, um die Dinge zu hinterfragen, auch einen distanzierten und kritischen Ansatz. Man müsse die eigene Meinung in die Arbeit einbringen.

Gemeinsamkeiten, Affinitäten im Gesamten wie im Detail: Plečniks ebenso eigenwillige wie beeindruckende Herz-Jesu-Kirche in Prag, ihre überraschenden Innenräume (der saalartig weite, streng gegliederte Hauptraum von geradezu klassizistischer Aussage, die tonnengewölbte, eher gedrungene Unterkirche, die an Revolutionsarchitektur erinnert, an Boulleé, an Gilly oder an den frühen Weinbrenner, der hoch aufragende, hell durchlichtete Rampenraum im Turmmassiv), die Gestaltung der Außenwände mit ihren Einschlüssen (oder die der National- und Universitätsbibliothek in Ljubljana) – die Ansätze sind vergleichbar: Tesars Großform, die der Klosterneuburger Kirche, des Synagogenprojekts für Dresden oder die der Kirche in der Donau City, ihre unverwechselbaren Innenräume, die Behandlung der Wandflächen, die Einkerbungen in der Schömerhaus-Fassade, die Öffnungen in Wand und Dach der Kirche in Klosterneuburg (die Fenster sind und Einschlüsse zugleich), die Bullaugen und die Bohrungen in den Wänden der Kirche in der Donau City – Gemeinsamkeiten und Affinitäten nicht als Abbild dessen, was gemacht, sondern als Abbild dessen, was gesucht wurde, im Sinne von Novalis: »Vergänglich ist nichts, was die Geschichte ergriff, aus unzähligen Verwandlungen geht es in immer reicheren Gestaltungen erneut wieder hervor.«

Es führt ein Weg vom Wiener Barock, von Hildebrandts Peterskirche und Fischer von Erlachs Karlskirche über Karl Friedrich Schinkel zu Otto Wagner und weiter zu Tesars Kirche: Hildebrandts konzentrierter Zentralbau mit den raumbeherrschenden vier »durchlöcherten« Pfeilermassiven, denen außen die »Vernadelung« der Hauptfassade durch zwei schräg gestellte Türme entspricht; Fischers Zentralbau mit vergleichbaren inneren durchlichteten Pfeilergruppen, denen außen an der Rückseite nahezu freigestellte, an der Eingangsseite weit nach außen gezogene Eckblöcke pylonenartig antworten; Schinkels Potsdamer Nikolaikirche, deren quadratischer Grundriß, deren kubischer Block innen durch mächtige, geschlossene Eckpfeiler gefaßt ist (über die die Lasten aus der Kuppel abgeleitet werden), die Schinkel außen aber nicht zeigen, über die er die Fassade ungebrochen einheitlich hinweglaufen lassen wollte (und die erst durch Persius' Veränderungen sichtbar gemacht wurden); Otto Wagners Kirche am Steinhof, deren Inneres ebenfalls durch – scheinbar – mächtige, geschlossene Eckmassive geprägt ist, die aber nur eingezogene (und in den Ecken verstärkte) Wände sind und die dieses Nur-Eingezogene, dieses Nicht-Massive außen auch vorgeben; Tesars Bau schließlich mit seinen signifikanten Eckausbildungen, die durch große Öffnungen außen und innen zeigen, was sie sind.

Es führt ein Weg von Rudolf Schwarz' so unerbittlich streng wirkender Aachener Fronleichnamskirche über seine Dürener Kirche St. Anna mit ihren beiden geschlossenen, imposanten Bruchsteinwänden zu Tesars Quader; es führt ein Weg von Franz Füegs ockerfarben durchlichteter Meggener Piuskirche zu Tesar, ein Weg von Eiermanns Kirchenbauten und -projekten, die nach einem einmal als gültig erachteten Prinzip, der von einer Lichthülle umgebenen Halle, konzipiert sind, ein Weg von Schwarz' Antoniuskirche in Essen zu Tesar, auch eine Art »Kreuzquader«, in der nicht der Quader dominiert mit einspringenden Ecken, sondern – umgekehrt – die Kreuzform, die in einen Sockel einsinkt; es führt ein Weg von Carlo Scarpas ebenso schlichtem wie kunstvoll-raffiniert belichtetem Erweiterungsbau des Canova-Museums in Possagno nach Wien – zu einer eigenständigen modernen, einer schönen Architektur ohne kurzlebige Trompetenfanfaren architektonischer Geistesblitze, zu einer Architektur wie die der Kirche Christus Hoffnung der Welt führen viele Wege, denen nachzugehen, sich selbst sichtbar zu machen, notwendig ist, weil man, wie Rudolf Schwarz es formuliert hat, »die Gegenwartsprobleme nur dann erkennen kann, wenn man in die ganze Tiefe seiner Tradition hinabtaucht, so, wie man auch den Wuchs eines Baumes nicht erkennen kann, wenn man ihn in irgendeiner Zeithöhe durchschneidet, sondern nur, wenn man ihn in seinem ganzen Wuchs bis in die Wurzeln sich vergegenwärtigt«.

24. Rudolf Schwarz, Fronleichnamskirche, Aachen, 1928–30.
25. Rudolf Schwarz, St. Anna, Düren, 1951–56.
26. Rudolf Schwarz, St. Antonius, Essen, 1956–59.
27. Jože Plečnik, Herz-Jesu-Kirche, Prag, 1928–33.
28. Otto Wagner, Kirche am Steinhof, Wien, 1904–07.
29. Carlo Scarpa, Erweiterung des Canova-Museums, Possagno, 1955–57.

24. Rudolf Schwarz, Fronleichnamskirche, Aachen, 1928–30.
25. Rudolf Schwarz, St. Anna, Düren, 1951–56.
26. Rudolf Schwarz, St. Antonius, Essen, 1956–59.
27. Jože Plečnik, Church of the Sacred Heart, Prague, 1928–33.
28. Otto Wagner, Kirche am Steinhof, Vienna, 1904 to 1907.
29. Carlo Scarpa, extension to the Canova Museum, Possagno, 1955–57.

wall and roof of the church in Klosterneuburg (which are windows and inclusions at the same time), the portholes and the drill-holes in the walls of the church in the Donau City – common features and affinities not just as an image of what has been done but as an image of what was sought, in the spirit of Novalis: »Nothing shall pass that history has seized, from countless transitions it emerges once more in ever richer creations.«

There is a path that leads from Viennese Baroque, from Hildebrandt's Peterskirche and Fischer von Erlach's Karlskirche via Karl Friedrich Schinkel to Otto Wagner and on to Tesar's church: Hildebrandt's concentrated central plan with the four space-dominating »perforated« pier massifs, with the corresponding exterior »pinning« of the main façade by two diagonally placed towers; Fischer's central plan with comparable groups of through-lit piers in the interior, to which corner blocks respond like pylons outside: almost freestanding behind the church, but drawn a long way outwards on the entrance side; Schinkel's Nikolaikirche in Potsdam, whose square ground plan, whose cubic block is framed in the interior by massive, closed corner piers (through which the load from the dome is dispersed), but that Schinkel did not want to show outside, wanting the façade to run over them uniformly unbroken (they were only revealed by Persius's alterations); Otto Wagner's Kirche am Steinhof, whose interior is also shaped by solid – apparently solid – closed corner massifs, though in fact they are only walls that have been pulled in (and reinforced at the corners); they also demonstrate that they are only pulled in, and not solid, outside the building; and finally Tesar's building, with its significantly developed corners, demonstrating what they are by means of large internal and external apertures.

There is a path that leads from Rudolf Schwarz's Fronleichnamskirche in Aachen, which seems so inexorably severe, via his Church of St. Anna in Düren with its two closed, impressive undressed stone walls to Tesar's cuboid; there is a path that leads from Franz Füeg's ochre-lit Piuskirche in Meggen, a path from Eiermann's churches and projects, conceived according to a principle that was once considered valid, the hall surrounded by a veil of light, there is a path that leads from Schwarz's Antoniuskirche in Essen to Tesar, also a kind of »cross cuboid«, in which the dominant feature is not the cuboid with its inset corners, but – conversely – the cross shape sinking into a plinth; there is a path that leads from Carlo Scarpa's extension to the Canova Museum in Passagno, which is as simple as it is artfully and subtly lit, to Vienna – to independent modern architecture, to beautiful architecture without architectural flashes of inspiration with their short-lived trumpet fanfares. There are many paths that lead to architecture like that of the church of Christ Hope of the World, and it is necessary to go down these paths, to make them visible for oneself, because, as Rudolf Schwarz has put it, we »can only recognize the problems of the present by plunging fully into the depths of its tradition, just as the growth of a tree cannot be recognized by cutting through it at some time-level, but only by imagining every aspect of its growth, down to the very roots«.

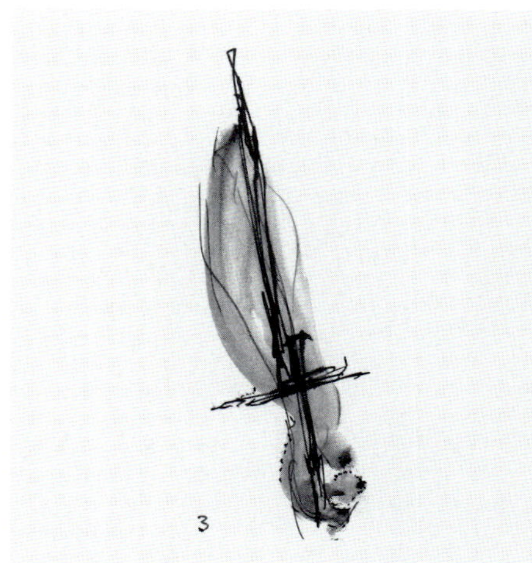
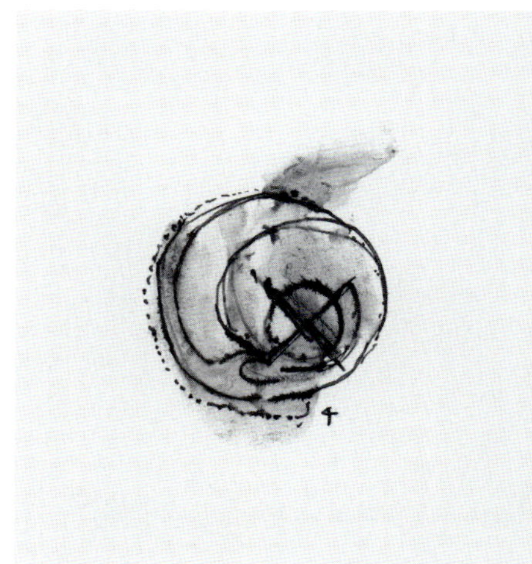
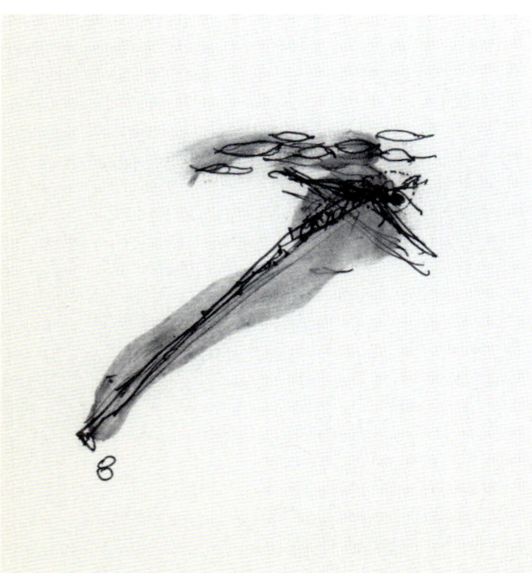
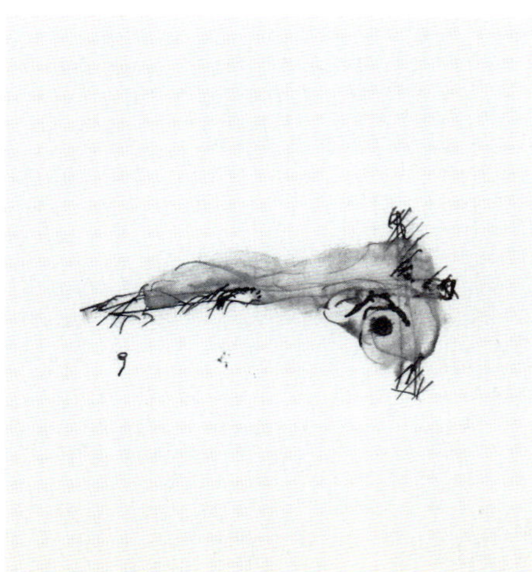
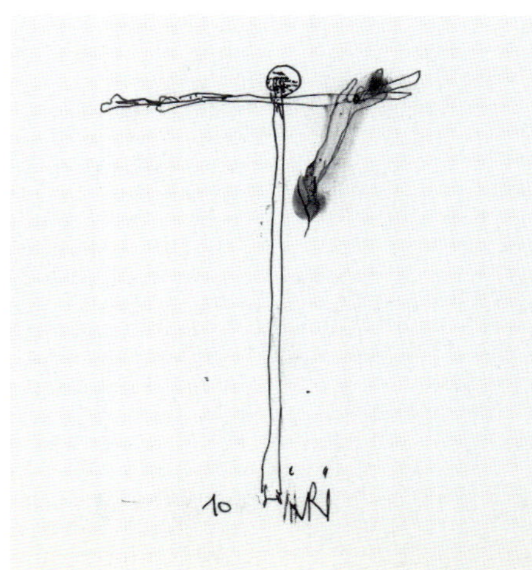
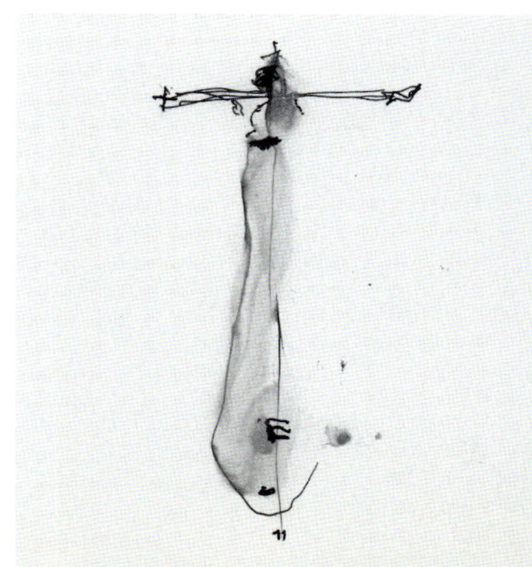

1–14. Heinz Tesar, *Kreuzwegstationen*, Siebdruck auf Leinen, 76 x 76 cm, 1998–2001. Dieses Werk wurde speziell für die Kirche geschaffen.

1–14. Heinz Tesar, *Stations of Cross*, screen printing on canvas, 76 x 76 cm, 1998–2001. This work was created especially for the church.

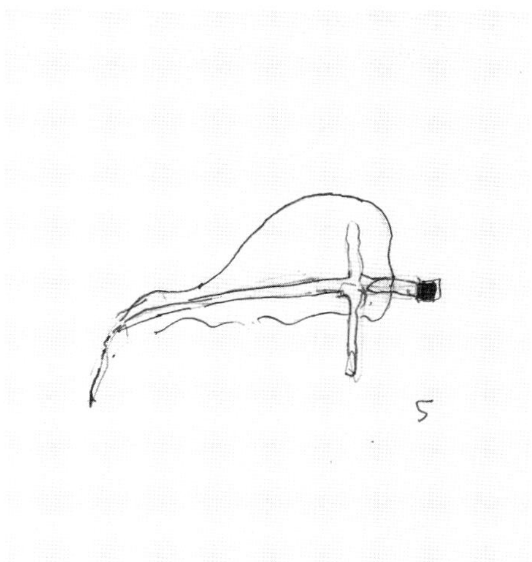

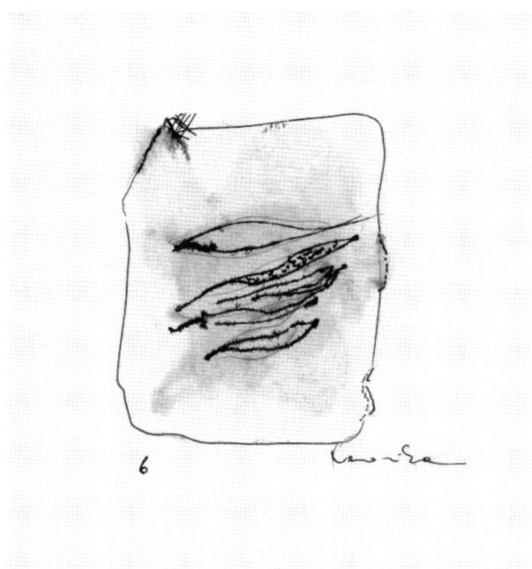

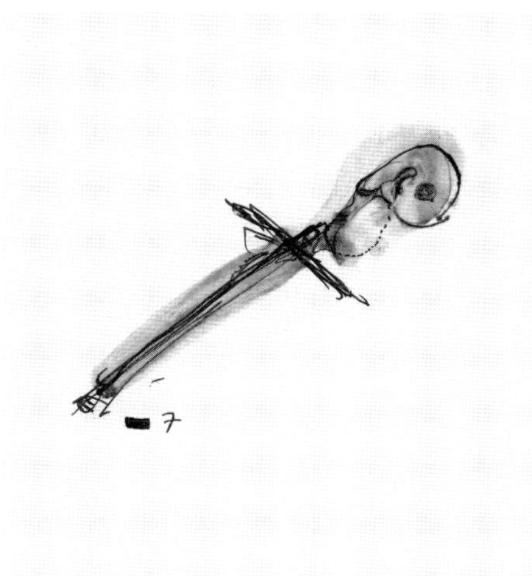

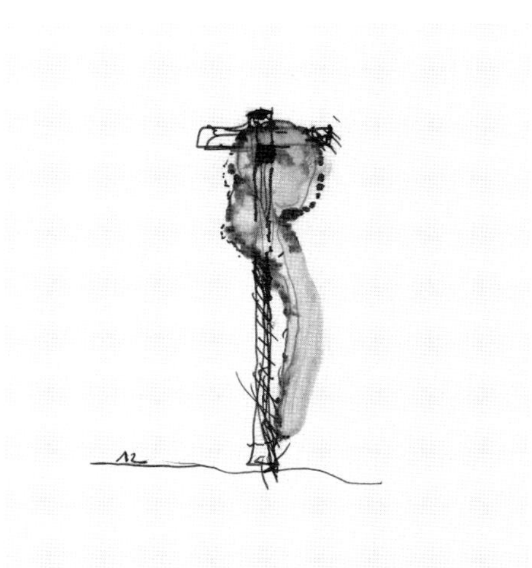

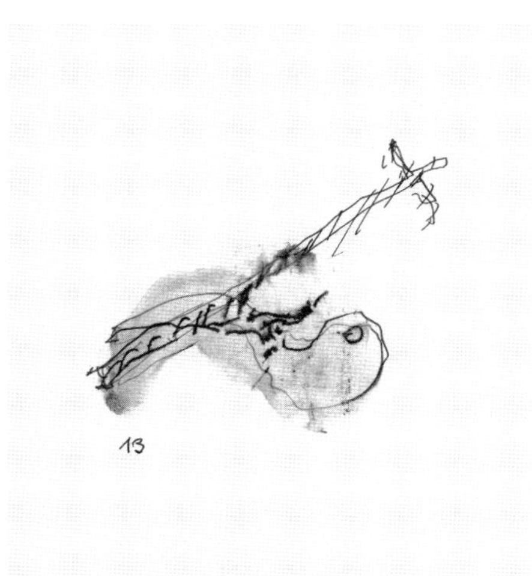

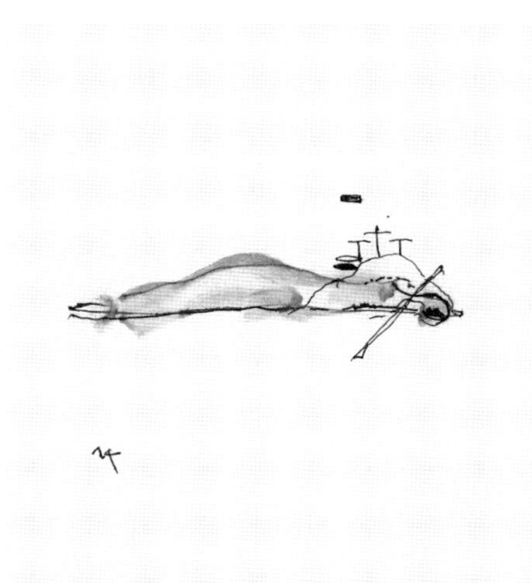

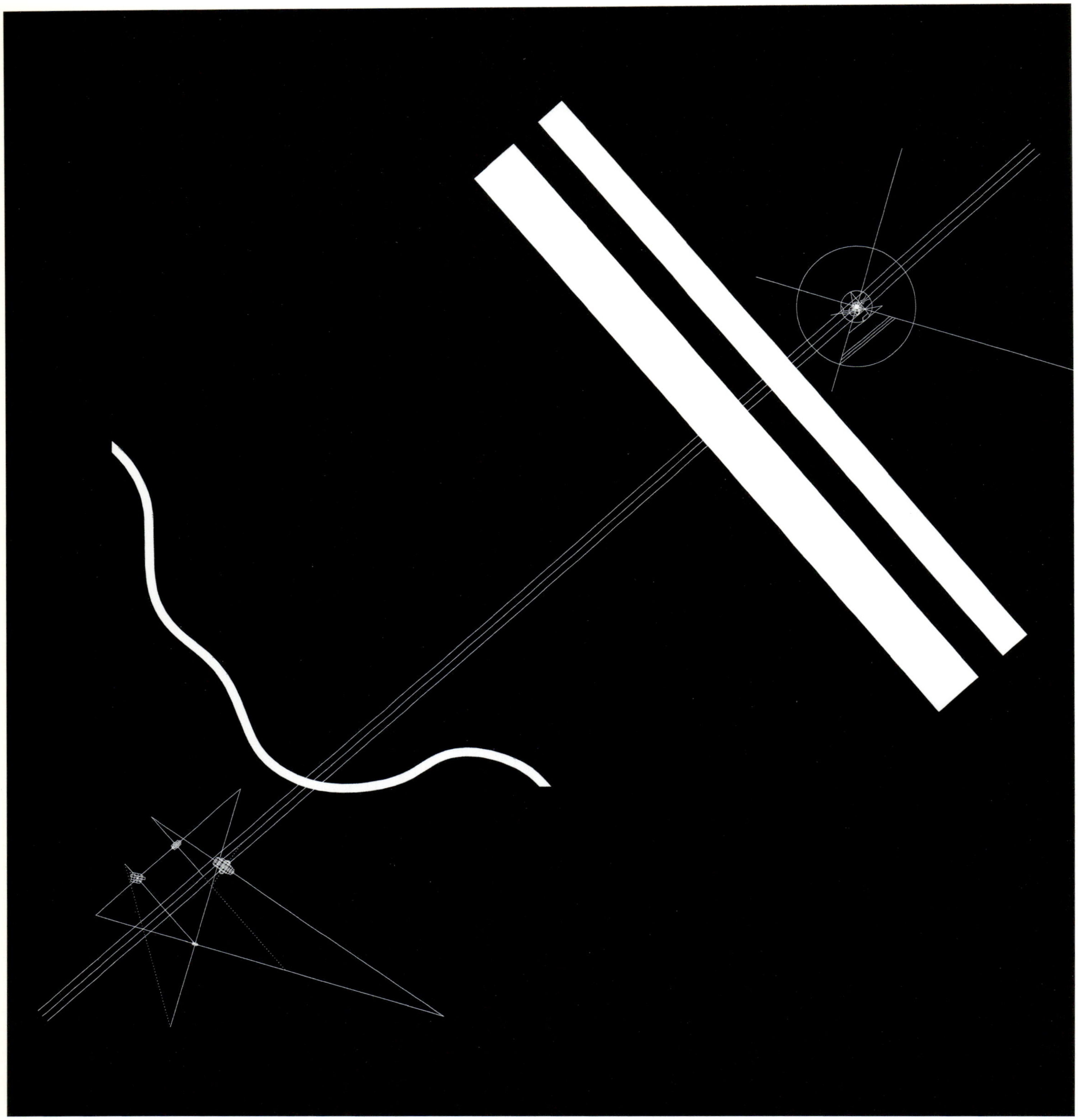

1. Die Kirche in ihrem städtebaulichen Kontext.
2. Lageplan.

1. The church in its urban context.
2. Site plan.

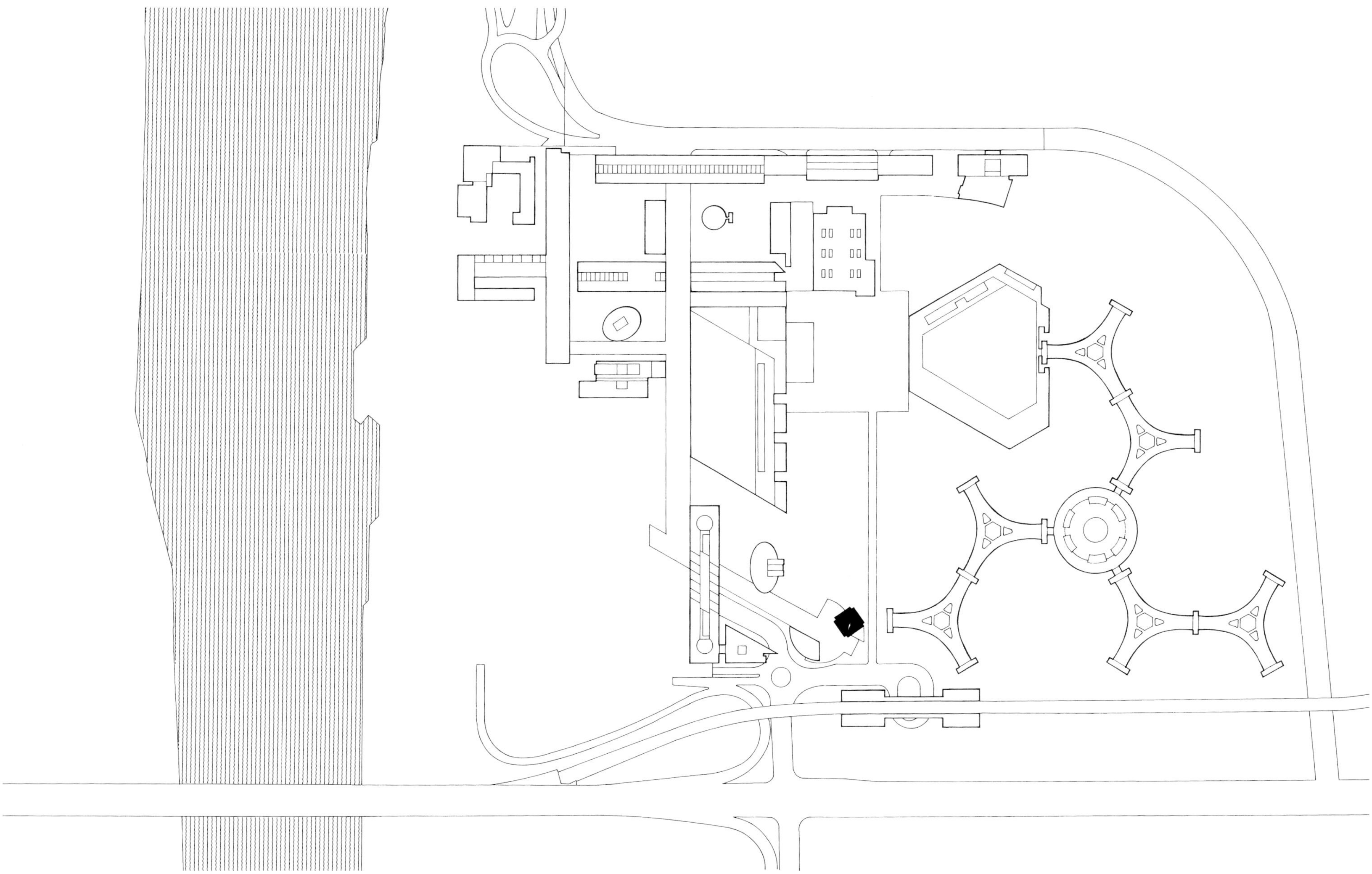

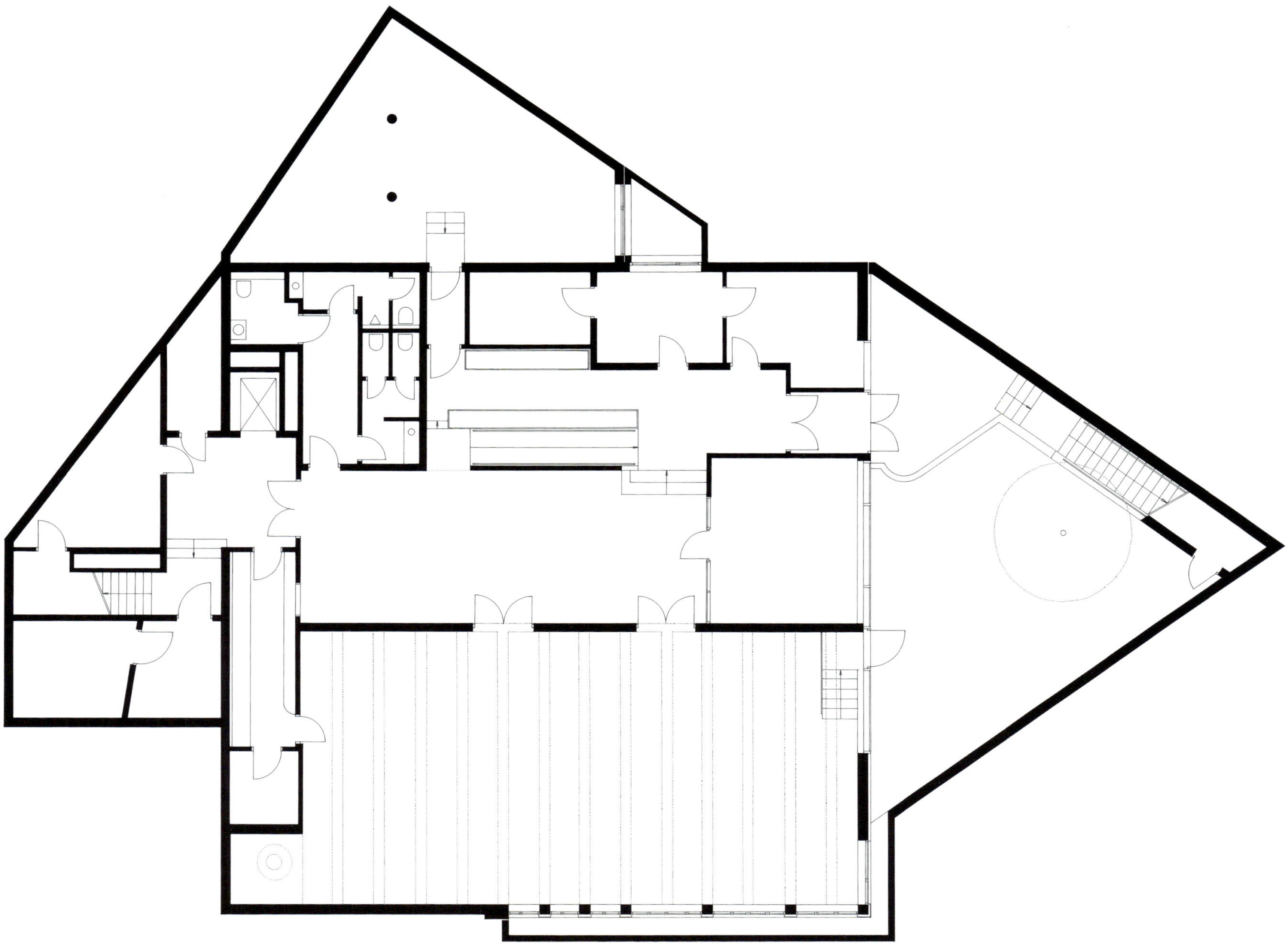

3, 4. Grundrisse.

3, 4. Floor plans.

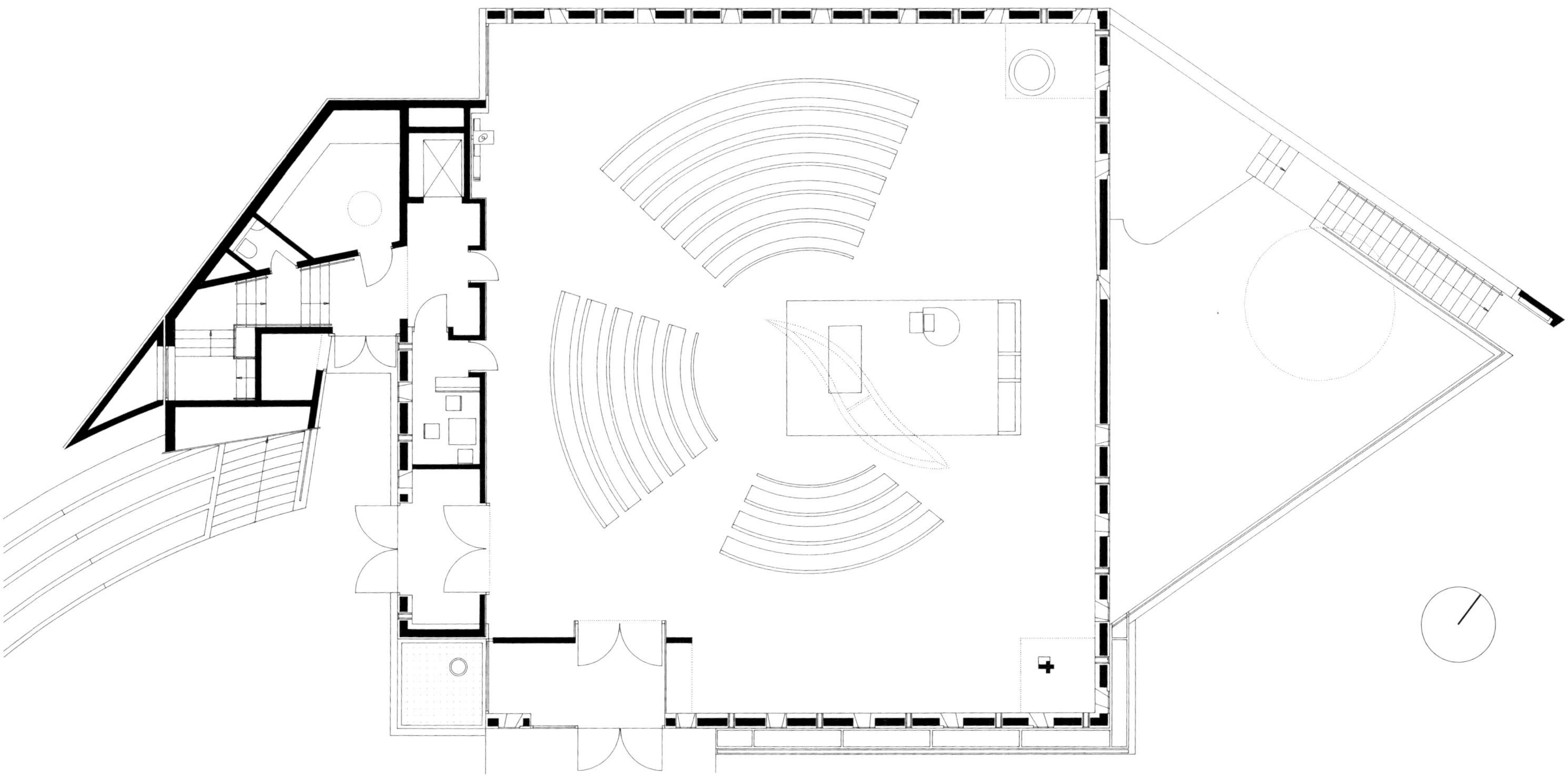

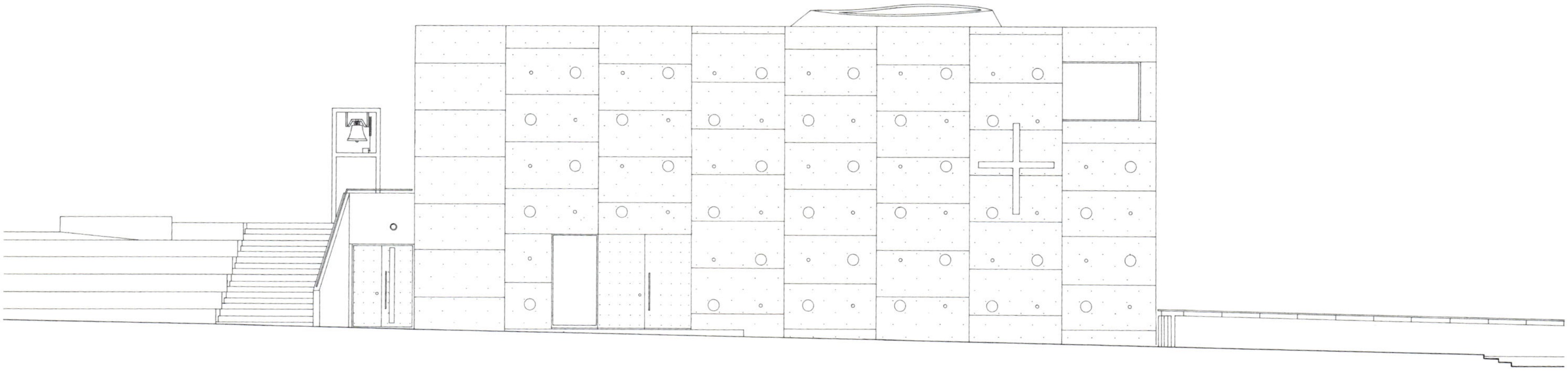

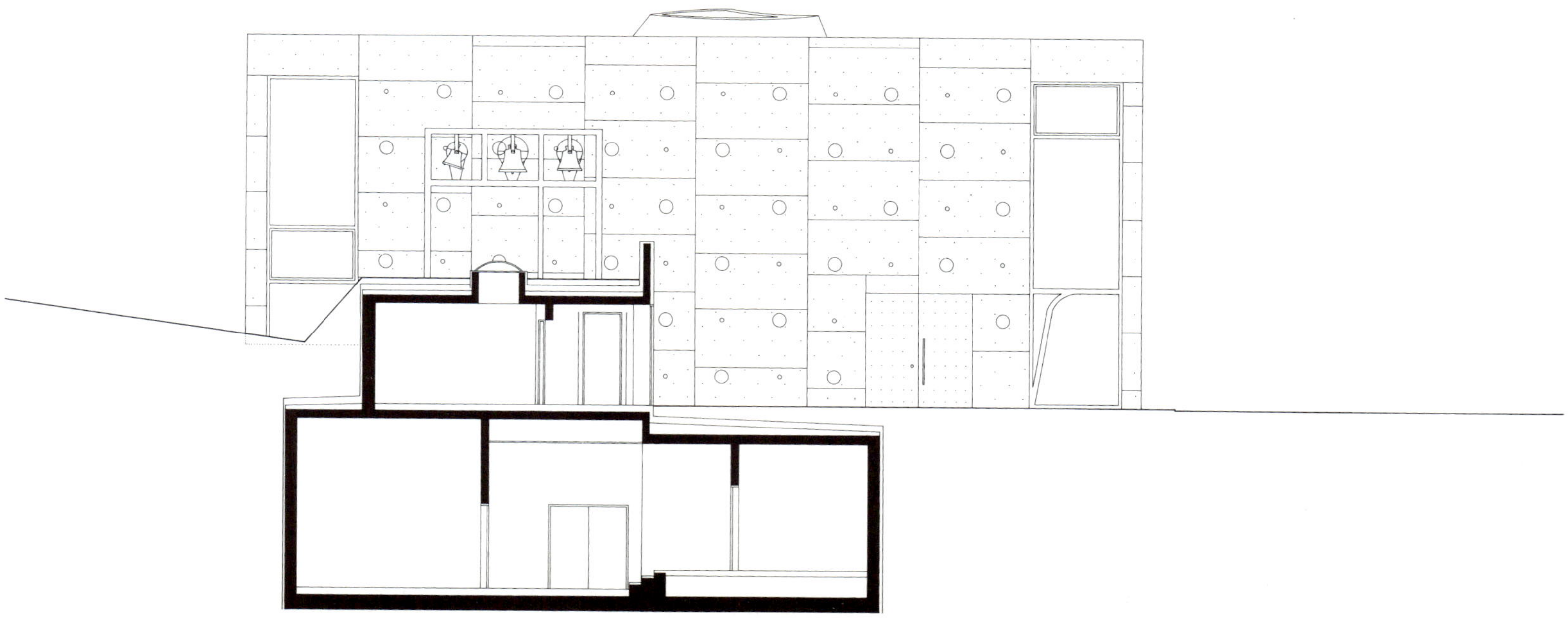

5. Aufriß von Südosten.
6–8. Schnitte.

5. Southeast elevation.
6–8. Sections.

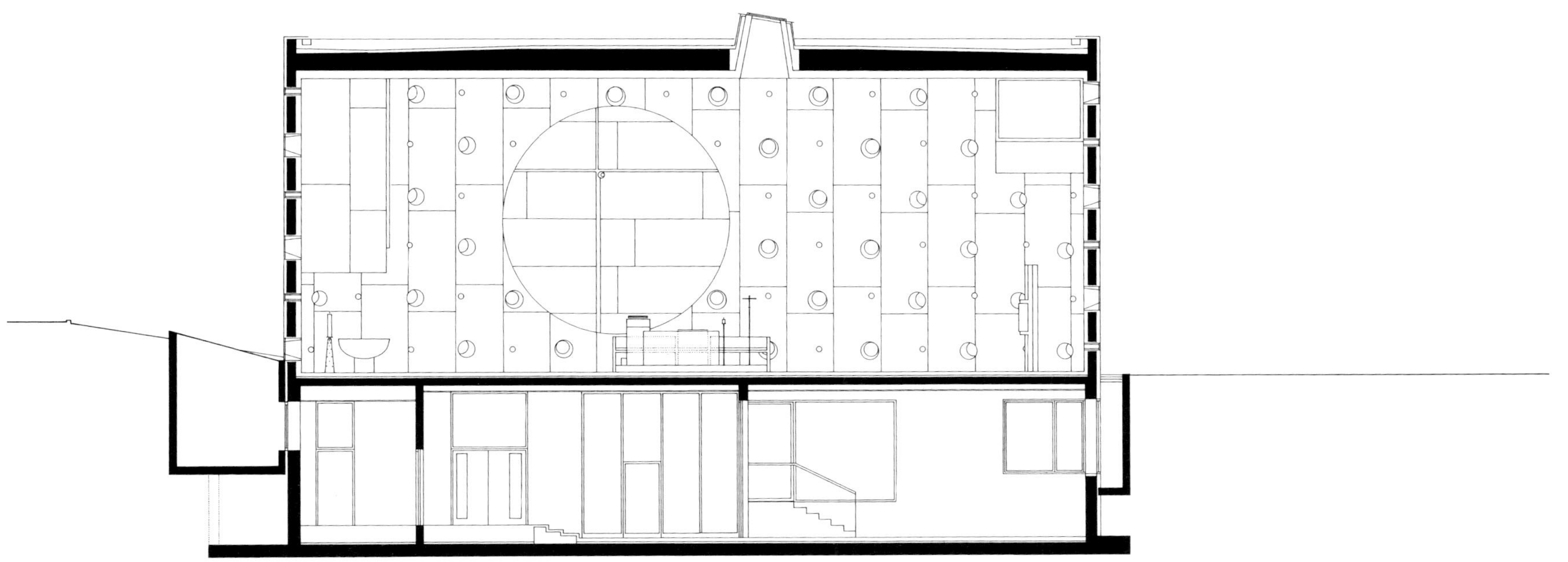

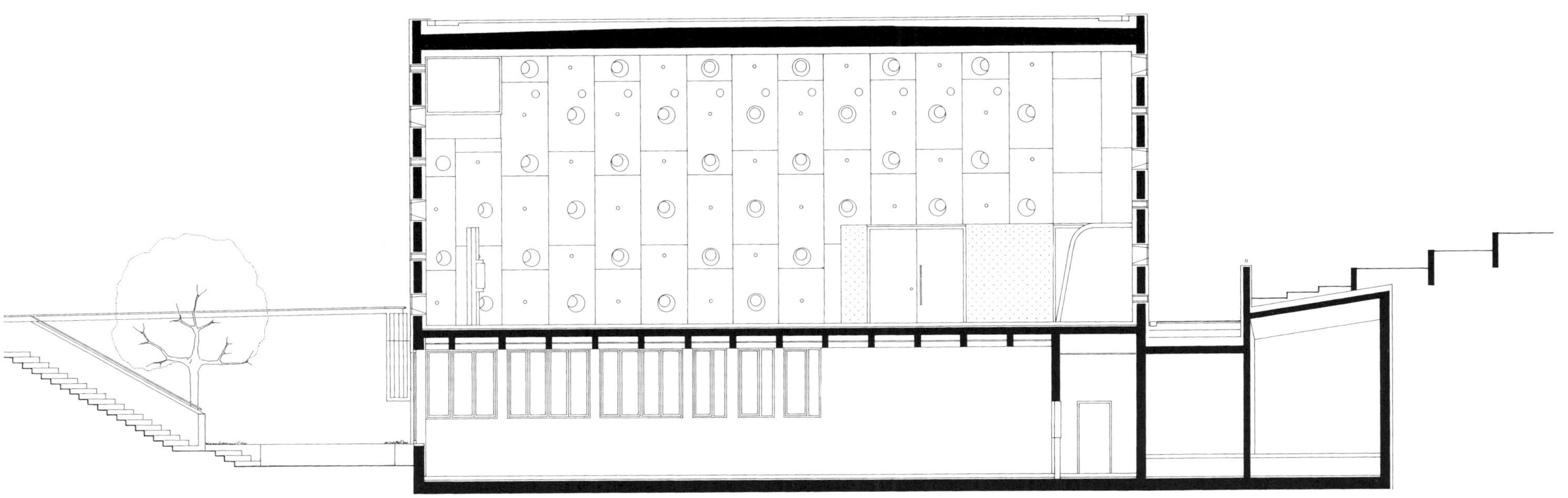

1. Luftaufnahme von Südosten.
2. Luftaufnahme von Nordwesten.

1. Aerial view from the southeast.
2. Aerial view from the northwest.

CINEPLEXX PALACE

3. Gesamtansicht von Südwesten.
4. Gesamtansicht von Nordosten.

3. General view from the southwest.
4. General view from the northeast.

5. Gesamtansicht von Osten.
6. Gesamtansicht von Süden.
7. Gesamtansicht von Südosten.

5. General view from the east.
6. General view from the south.
7. General view from the southeast.

S. 34/35
8. Gesamtansicht von Südwesten.

p. 34/35
8. General view from the southwest.

9. Gesamtansicht von Südosten.
10. Detailansicht von Osten.

9. General view from the southeast.
10. Detail view from the east.

11. Detailansicht von Südwesten.
12. Detailansicht von Nordosten.

11. Detail view from the southwest.
12. Detail view from the northeast.

13. Detailansicht der Nordostfassade.

13. Detail view of the northeast façade.

14. Detailansicht der Ostecke.

14. Detail view of the east corner.

S. 42/43
15. Blick von Südwesten in den Kirchenraum.

p. 42/43
15. View of the church interior from the southwest.

S. 44/45
16. Blick von Nordwesten in den Kirchenraum.

S. 44/45
16. View into the church interior from the northwest.

17. Eingangsbereich. Links der Haupteingang, rechts der Nebeneingang.
18. Eingangsbereich. Im Zentrum der Haupteingang, rechts der Nebeneingang.

17. Entrance area. The main entrance is to the left, the side entrance to the right.
18. Entrance area. The main entrance is in the centre, the side entrance to the right.

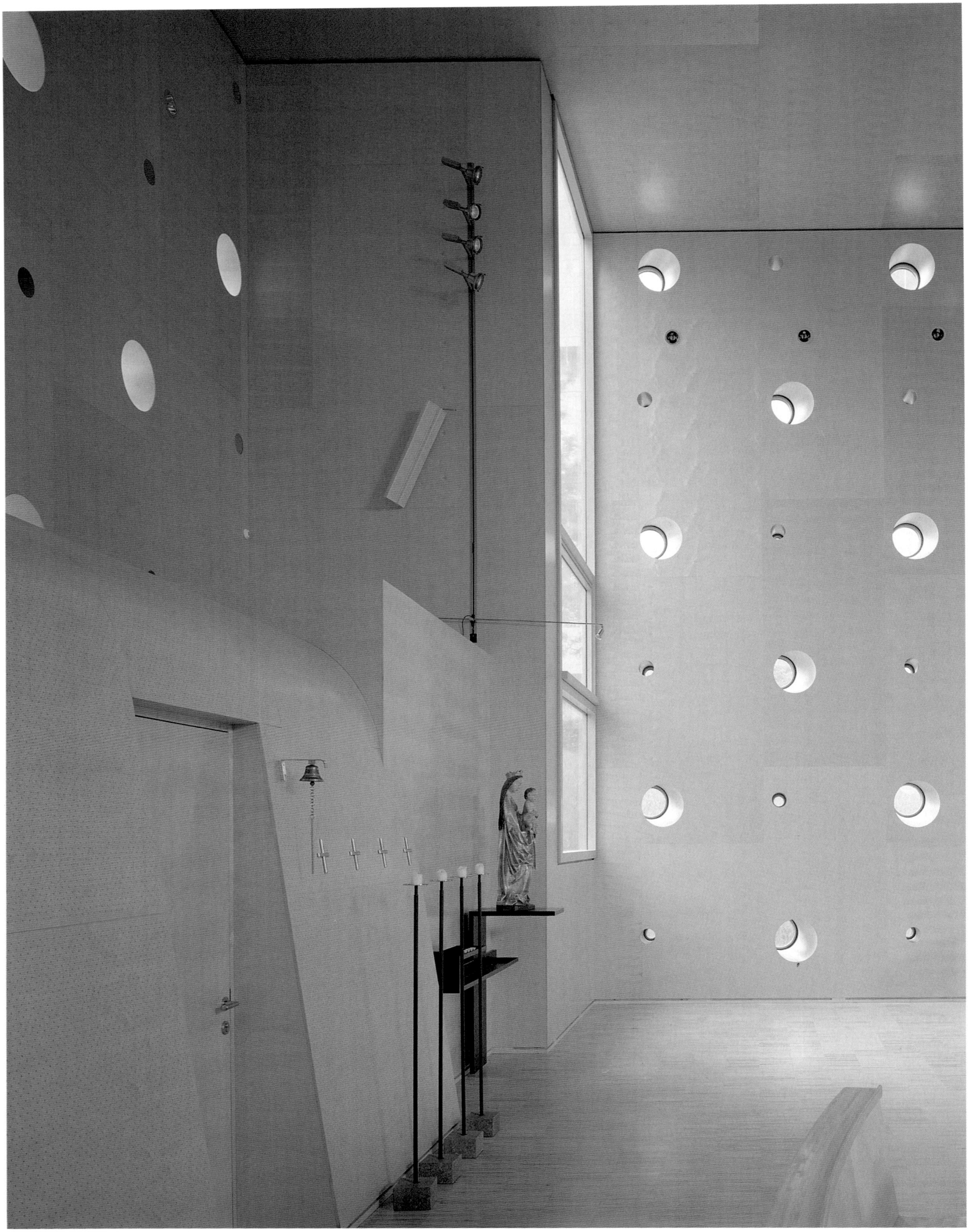

19. Die Marienstatue an der Südwestseite des Kirchenraums.

19. The statue of Maria on the southwest side of the church interior.

20. Der Tabernakel in der Ostecke der Kirche.

20. The tabernacle in in the east corner of the church interior.

21. Das Taufbecken in der Nordecke des Kirchenraums.
22. Der Altar.

21. The baptismal font in the north corner of the church interior.
22. The altar.

23, 24. Der Gemeindebereich im Untergeschoß der Kirche.
23, 24. The parish rooms in the basement of the church.

25. Der große Gemeindesaal.
26. Blick vom kleinen Gemeindesaal
in den abgesenkten Gartenhof.

25. The large parish hall.
26. View of the sunken garden courtyard
from the small parish hall.

Christus Hoffnung der Welt, Donau City, Wien

Wettbewerb / Competition
1997/98

Ausführung / Realisation
1999 / 2000

Bauherr / Client
Erzdiözese Wien, Erzbischöfliches Bauamt
(Harald Gnilsen)

Architekt
Heinz Tesar, Wien / Vienna, mit / with Marc Tesar
Projektleitung / Project management: Oliver Aschenbrenner
Mitarbeiter / Collaborators: Achim Bilger, Urs Geiger, Silvia Prager, Heidi Schatzl, Franz Steinberger, Susanne Veit

Örtliche Bauleitung / Site management
Sepp Müller, Wien / Vienna
Mitarbeiter: Gerhard Kogert

Statik / Statics
Arbeitsgemeinschaft Lindlbauer – Zehetner, Wien / Vienna

Haustechnik / Mechanical engineering
IC – Interdisziplinäre Consulenten Ziviltechniker Ges. m. b. H., Wien / Vienna

Bauphysik / Structural physics
Walter Prause, Wien / Vienna

Bauunternehmen / Main contractor
Steiner-Bau Ges. m. b. H., St. Paul im Lavanttal

Fassaden / Façades
Ing. A. Sauritschnig Alu – Stahl – Glas
Gesellschaft m. b. H., St. Veit an der Glan

Holzverkleidung / Timber cladding
Steinbacher & Sohn, Hollenstein an der Ybbs

Kirchenbänke / Pews
J. Arnauer, Sierndorf an der March

Photonachweis für den Essayteil / Photo credits for the essay part

Immo Boyken 10.4, 13.11, 15.15
Richard Bryant 19.29
Clemens Holzmeister, Salzburg / Leipzig 1937 13.10
Dominikus Böhm, München 1962 14.12
Egon Eiermann, 1904–1970, Stuttgart 1984 15.16
Egon Eiermann. Die Kaiser-Wilhelm-Gedächtnis-Kirche, Berlin 1994 10.3
Urs Geiger 8.2
Ludwig Hilberseimer, *Mies van der Rohe*, Chicago 1956 15.14
Jahrbuch 1988. Sonderforschungsbereich »Erhalten historisch bedeutsamer Bauwerke«, Berlin 1989 14.13
Jože Plečnik, Architekt, 1872–1957, München 1987 19.27
Otto Wagner. Das Werk des Wiener Architekten 1841 bis 1918, Darmstadt 1963 19.28
Christian Richters 16.19
Rudolf Schwarz, *Kirchenbau. Welt vor der Schwelle*, Heidelberg 1960 18.24, 18.25, 18.26
Hans Sedlmayr, *Johann Bernhard Fischer von Erlach*, Wien 1976 17.23
Margeritha Spiluttini 16.18
Wasmuths Monatshefte für Baukunst, 1929/6 8.1
Wasmuths Monatshefte für Baukunst, 1933/5 15.17